Young Architects 9

Young Architects 9

PROOF

Foreword by Sarah Whiting
Introduction by Anne Rieselbach

ludens

PRODUCTORA

PARA

Jinhee Park

Aranda/Lasch

UNI

PRINCETON ARCHITECTURAL PRESS
THE ARCHITECTURAL LEAGUE OF NEW YORK

Published by
Princeton Architectural Press
37 East 7th Street, New York, New York 10003

For a free catalog of books, call 1.800.722.6657.
Visit our website at www.papress.com

To view podcast interviews with each firm please
visit the Architectural League's website at
www.archleague.org

This publication is made possible with public funds
from the New York State Council on the Arts,
a state agency.

State of the Arts

NYSCA

Editor: Linda Lee
Designer: Paul Wagner

Special thanks to:
Nettie Aljian, Sara Bader, Dorothy Ball, Nicola Bednarek,
Janet Behning, Becca Casbon, Penny (Yuen Pik) Chu,
Russell Fernandez, Pete Fitzpatrick, Wendy Fuller, Jan Haux,
Clare Jacobson, Aileen Kwun, Nancy Eklund Later,
Laurie Manfra, Katharine Myers, Lauren Nelson Packard,
Jennifer Thompson, Arnoud Verhaeghe, Joseph Weston,
and Deb Wood of Princeton Architectural Press
—Kevin C. Lippert, publisher

Library of Congress Cataloging-in-Publication Data
Proof / foreword by Sarah Whiting ; introduction by
Anne Rieselbach.
        p.   cm.
— (Young architects ; 9)
ISBN 978-1-56898-743-9 (pbk. : alk. paper)
1. Young Architects Forum. 2. Architecture—Awards—
United States. 3. Architecture—United States—21st
century. 4. Young architects—United States.
I. Architectural League of New York.
NA2340.Y6797 2008
720.79'73—dc22

                                  2007036763

Contents

Acknowledgments 9
Foreword, Sarah Whiting 10
Introduction, Anne Rieselbach 13
Biographies 16

Iudens 20

PRODUCTORA 46

PARA 72

Jinhee Park 100

Aranda/Lasch 126

UNI 152

The Architectural League of New York
Board of Directors

Acknowledgments
Calvin Tsao, President
The Architectural League of New York

Proof was the Architectural League's twenty-sixth annual Young Architects Forum competition. Open to architects and designers who are ten years or less out of undergraduate or graduate school, this annual portfolio competition continues to recognize and provide a significant platform to promising young architects. Participants are given the opportunity to create site-specific installations of their work, present lectures at the League's Young Architects Forum, participate in video podcast interviews, as well as publish their work for this annual catalog.

Each year the Young Architects Committee, composed of past Young Architects Forum participants, identifies a theme or concept for the competition. Its members, along with prominent members of the architecture and design community, serve as jurors.

I am delighted to have this opportunity to thank committee members David Benjamin, Daniel D'Oca, and Lisa Hsieh, as well as my fellow jurors Michael Bell, Toshiko Mori, and Sarah Whiting, who has also written a thoughtful foreword to this publication. I also want to thank Michael Bierut and Jena Sher for the competition graphics and Adam Mosseri, who transformed and animated their graphic language for installation onto the League's website. Once again, photographer David Sundberg gave his time to document the exhibition.

The Young Architects Forum is made possible in part by the generous support of Artemide Inc., Hunter Douglas, Dornbracht, Susan Grant Lewin Associates, 3form, and Tischler und Sohn. The League's programs are also made possible in part by public funds from the New York City Department of Cultural Affairs and the New York State Council on the Arts, a State Agency. Finally, we also gratefully wish to acknowledge the support of the LEF Foundation for the Young Architects Forum video podcasts and this publication.

Foreword
Sarah Whiting, Assistant Professor of History and Theory,
Princeton University School of Architecture;
Partner, WW Architecture

"The proof is in the pudding." Proving that my gastronomic genes completely outnumber my mathematical ones, this saying kept running through my head when jurying the Architectural League's Young Architects Forum competition this past February. If the proof is in the pudding—which I imagined to be like the *fève* (a bean or a porcelain figure) buried inside the delicious frangipane-filled Galettes des Rois eaten throughout France on Epiphany (whoever gets the fève becomes royalty for a year)—then, despite the Young Architects Committee's protests to the contrary in the competition brief, proof is in fact *product* as much as it is *process*: it's the *demonstration*, meaning the end product, as well as the action of *demonstrating*.

How do you find the fève in a pile of portfolios? What even constitutes architectural proof for a young office today? The brilliance of the concise Young Architects Forum competition title is that it encourages focus, punch, and precision. The risk of the very same is that a one-word title often ends up fighting its own pithiness by embracing a degree of ambiguity, fluidity, and multifariousness. The seemingly scientific—and therefore seemingly inherently precise—"Proof" does not avoid this trap, and perhaps that's because it, like much of architecture today, originated in committee, which necessarily dilutes precision. In the competition brief, proof is invoked as hypothesis, as experiment, as demonstration, as conceptual, as material, as technological, as structural. The first fève-test, then, was how the provocative proof was articulated within the entrant's portfolio. It was, frankly, disappointing to see how few entrants successfully engaged the topic; it was even more disappointing to see that even fewer submitted portfolios that simply looked good. In an era where even Kmart—or at least Martha Stewart—manages to promote simple, clean aesthetics, how is it that so many people less than ten years out of architecture school cannot design a portfolio? The six selected fèves looked good and said something.

"Proof calls for creativity at a conceptual level, but also demands innovation in the ways we activate and employ our concepts" was the most telling phrase in the call for entries. Given the constraints of economy and experience, practice today requires a remarkable degree of agility. One cannot envision a proof and then simply produce it—the proof or product has to evolve with the process. At the same time, without an envisioned project, there is no proof to be had. The biggest challenge today for young—and even not-so-young—architects is to have a project in mind and to maintain it when carrying out a commission. All too often there is a divide between an office's competition work, which focuses and promotes ideas and agendas, and "real" work, which merely solves problems.

While the six selected winners differ greatly, a general shared optimism wafts across the entire group, complemented by quick wit, which often helps to push optimism toward ambition rather than letting it remain in the realm of mere naïveté. Aranda/Lasch's Monty Python–esque Victorian cartoon figures peopling the elegant renderings of their Grotto entry for the P.S.1 competition reveal the breadth of their references and intended audience. PARA's Photoshopped nip and tuck of Mies's face as a segue to manipulations of the Seagram facade offers a simple, effective, and droll snapshot into what makes 2007 so different from 1958. While entirely speculative, the project reveals the firm's interest in tweaking, optimizing, and differentiating rather than standardizing. Similarly, Jinhee Park's softened typologies—the soft perimeter of the Williamsburg Lofts and the curtains that turn rooms into parentheses in the HBNY project—offer maybe not a witty but certainly a relaxed and agile approach to modern life. PRODUCTORA, on the other hand, the entry who had the most work among all of the competitors, reveals its optimism not so much through wit as through sheer production.

The optimism underlying UNI's decision to "borrow to the hilt" and "do it all"—from developing to constructing their four-unit condominium project in Cambridge, Massachusetts, for example—reveals how fine a line lies between youthful optimism and insane risk. Such risk, or willingness to redefine the limits of practice, may be the only way that small, young firms can achieve any recognition, let alone work. The firm ludens from Mexico City has opted for another, more guerilla tactic for its practice of small installations that take over the city and/or domestic life—in the Segregator project, for example, a mobile security gate creates checkpoints at any given spot.

The year 2007 is hardly a moment in an era of optimism. "Inconvenient truths" are no longer possible to ignore and lack of truths pepper our political terrain. This competition's proof of different possible optimisms is a remarkable reminder that the future can indeed remain bright. The full adage reads: "The proof of the pudding is in the eating." Looks like we'll be eating well for a while yet.

Introduction
Anne Rieselbach, Program Director
The Architectural League of New York

Creating architecture involves testing and reconciling many variables—ideally making the theoretical real and the pragmatic transcendent. The Architectural League's Young Architects Committee conceived the theme "Proof" to challenge entrants to consider how the conceptual processes and empirical methods inherent in the term "proof" shape their own architectural projects, specifically, what happens to the development of their design when "work meets world."

Within this realm of conceptual testing, the committee defined "architectural projects" as trial sheets subject to constant review and change, as transcripts of dialogues among multiple parties that record our forward, backward, and lateral movement across the territory of the proof. Entrants were encouraged to consider how they carried out a design proof. They were to consider sources, variables, and ways of visually interpreting abstract constructs. More specific to design were the questions: How do we tackle sub-proofs, such as conceptual proof, material proof, technological proof, and structural proof? How do we balance innovation and independence with partnership and consensus? How do we anticipate an unknown future? As the work is open-ended, how do we know when to stop? When do we consider a project finished?

The ways in which the competition winners chose to display their work was telling, emphasizing process and product. In some cases their choices posed open-ended questions that pointed more toward new experiments than resolutions, while others ordered wildly different variables to create singular forms.

Ivan Hernandez Quintela, principal of ludens, placed full-scale pieces throughout the galleries. Primarily scaled to the human body, his work explores "how objects and spaces tend to affect one's behavior by becoming interactive mechanisms, capable of being transformed by their use." Some of his designs test ways of generating movement or achieving a tenuous, temporary stability, others ways of documenting movement and path. The different-sized pockets attached to the Collector's Garment are intended to receive "evidence" from city walks. Other work kinetically occupies space, forcing users to create their own means of stability. The teeter-totter-like structure of Unstable Obstacle, a "collective bench," requires negotiation between occupants to maintain its balance. The pinwheel-propelled Restless Chair theoretically moves with the wind to seek its own occupants—completing a cycle of urban restlessness.

In contrast, PRODUCTORA partners Carlos Bedoya, Wonne Ickx, Victor Jaime, and Abel Perles chose to compactly display ten schematic project models on a simple, elevated white field. Their buildings nestled almost enigmatically into a terraced landscape. The firm intentionally avoided using photographs and presentation or study models, challenging their capacity to accurately convey architectural space. Instead, their intention was to create "an imaginative landscape of objects [that] talks about space, texture, material, composition, distribution, and scale rather than about the...specific projects." The firm's work ranges in size from installation designs and small domestic and commercial projects to more urban-scaled competition entries. The collapsing of scale in the exhibition afforded the viewer the opportunity to understand and compare the basic elements of and formal relationships between each project.

Surfaced with an overscaled Rorschach inkblot test, a twelve-foot-by-twelve-foot "folded" reflective wall framed the installation designed by PARA partners Dominic Leong, Jonathan Lott, and Brian Price. A repetitive pattern of ten iconic buildings was intended to provide a field for questioning "both image and context," lending multiple readings for the familiar and foreign. PARA's work frequently manipulates surface and pattern to create a catalyst for both literal and speculative reflection. Reflective surfaces also enliven their scheme for the Times Square Military Lifestyle Center, creating an unlikely juxtaposition of a funhouse with an underlying military motif. Bordering their display were before-and-after portraits of Ludwig Mies van der Rohe, a startling transformation of the architect's familiar craggy visage, which provided a metaphor and starting point for, 'Lifting Mies, a speculative "plastic surgery" that modulates the Seagram Building's iconic gridded surface.

An undulating bent-wood schematic model of SINGLE speed DESIGN (SsD) partner Jinhee Park's Asian Cultural Complex for Gwangju, Korea, snaked around the installation, both housing project flip books and providing seating to view images suspended behind a translucent screen. This multivalent integration of program and form captured Park's integrative approach to urban design—which intentionally layers "interdisciplinary systems into a complex whole." Like Park and her partner John Hong's prizewinning Big Dig Building housing, which proposed reclaiming discarded infrastructure to undergird and frame new forms of urban housing, the Asian Cultural Complex recalls the optimistic age of megastructures designed to house fully the complexities of urban living. Both schemes weave commercial, recreational, and domestic elements to create a richly textured living complex.

Benjamin Aranda and Chris Lasch of Aranda/Lasch "splattered" a variegated collection of subtly toned vinyl wall graphics across the Urban Center's existing McKim, Mead, and White walls, "riding the surface of the mirrored wall, over and on to the moldings and turning the corners." The simple line drawings enigmatically represented fragments of the firm's projects, including their proposed Grotto for the MoMA/P.S.1 Young Architects Program, 10-Mile Spiral, and Baskets. Accompanying the exhibition was a small limited-edition portfolio that further detailed each project, revealing the full form and field of each work.

Frequently, young architects' own homes provide their first laboratories to test design strategies and gain hands-on construction experience—often with great economic and design risks. Taking this practice to the extreme, Chaewon Kim and Beat Schenk, partners of the firm UNI, wore almost every possible hat—from owner and developer to architect and contractor—to create their own home and three freestanding condominium units ranging in size from 1,100 to 2,400 square feet on a 12,000-square-foot lot in Cambridge, Massachusetts. The architects' display wall of photographs revealed the painstaking pairing of gut renovation with new construction. The finished complex is characterized by complementary but contrasting forms and materials—from a Cor-Ten steel–clad saltbox to a residence comprising three "stacked" and rotated okume wood–sided "boxes" connected by a plywood-encased stair.

Proof, as defined by the Young Architects Committee, is "process, not product." The work on display evoked an active sense of ongoing experimentation and invention. New materials, technology, and modes of practice meet traditional craft and building to provide unexpected sites for inquiry when architects, in the words of the call for entries, "work on proofs, put proof to work, witness the results, then rework the proofs."

Biographies

Ivan Hernandez Quintela is the founder and principal of **ludens** (www.ludens
.com.mx), a design firm established in 2002 in Mexico City. Since its inception
ludens has been investigating issues of intimacy and interaction in the public
and private spheres through the production of small-scale mechanisms.
Hernandez Quintela received his Bachelor of Architecture from the University
of Texas at Austin in 1999 and has been teaching at the Universidad
Iberoamericana in Mexico City since 2000.

PRODUCTORA is a Mexico City–based office founded in 2006. Its founding
members are **Abel Perles** (Argentina), **Carlos Bedoya** (Mexico), **Victor Jaime**
(Mexico), and **Wonne Ickx** (Belgium). Their individual educational backgrounds
and professional experiences give the studio a diverse approach to each
assignment. PRODUCTORA develops its ideas through intuitive explorations and
continuous production rather than adherence to an established strategy of
development. Therefore, the name PRODUCTORA—which is Spanish for producer
or production company—indicates production as a testing method.

PARA founders **Brian Price**, **Jonathan Lott**, and **Dominic Leong** liken their
practice to a think tank rather than an artistic quest, affirming that the production
of ideas is closely linked to the discourse of ideas. Their first projects were
conferences, addressing the current role of design research within the discipline
("PARAtheses," 2006) and opportunistic ways of practicing architecture
("Loopholes," 2005). Leong received a Master of Science in Advanced
Architectural Design from Columbia University Graduate School of Architecture,
Planning, and Preservation. Lott and Price each have a Master of Architecture
from Harvard University Graduate School of Design.

Jinhee Park received a Master of Architecture from the Harvard University
Graduate School of Design and a Bachelor of Fine Arts in industrial design
from Seoul National University. In 2001 she formed SsD (SINGLE speed DESIGN)
with her partner, John Hong, through which they explore the relationships
between architectural, industrial, and urban designs.

Park has received multiple prestigious design awards, including AIA/BSA honor awards, the Holcim Award for Sustainable Construction, and the Metropolis Next Generation Prize. Her work has been featured in major media such as *Metropolis* magazine, *Architectural Record*, *New Yorker*, *Dwell* magazine, and the PBS sustainable architecture television series *design: e²*, among others. Her academic appointments include the 2007 Sasaki Distinguished Visiting Critic at the Boston Architectural College, and she has lectured and exhibited at numerous universities and conferences. Park is a registered architect.

Benjamin Aranda and **Chris Lasch**, after meeting at school, founded two companies: terraswarm and **Aranda/Lasch**. It was important to have a second company so that, as architects, the two could have a dedicated outlet to not do architecture projects. Aranda/Lasch is dedicated to the production of space, while terraswarm is used to produce media projects. But this division is forced, and worse—after a few of the later projects—remains unclear. What is clear is that Aranda/Lasch have designed a Grotto, some baskets, which were a collaboration with Native American basket weaver Terrol Dew Johnson, and also a 10-Mile Spiral. Terraswarm has attached video cameras to birds and replaced the advertising feed on the country's largest video billboard with slowly changing but very bright colors.

UNI is a design/build company founded by **Chaewon Kim** and **Beat Schenk** in Cambridge, Massachusetts, in 2003. The firm acts simultaneously as architect, builder, owner, and developer, seeking innovative design solutions within the limitations of existing economic and zoning pressures. The company's most recent projects include S, M, L, XS: four houses—either renovated or newly built on a small lot in Cambridge—that test and explore design solutions to housing problems with affordable and sustainable materials. The innovative project has been widely published.

Kim and Schenk both received Bachelor of Architecture degrees from Southern California Institute of Architecture (SCI-Arc). Kim received her Master of Architecture degree from Harvard University Graduate School of Design, and Schenk received his Master of Architecture degree from Columbia University.

ludens

22   **Public Support**
24   **The Segregator**
25   **Birdhouses**
26   **Unstable Obstacle**
28   **Urban Oasis**
32   **Information Center**
34   **Public Mobile Library**
36   **Reading Room**
38   **Scaffolding Room**
40   **Collector's Studio**
42   **Sliding Table**
43   **Seesaw Table**
44   **Mexican Army Shelf**

TOOLS FOR EVERYDAY LIVING

The following projects are a series of exercises that examine the conditions of intimacy. Each project, devised as a tool, explores the many ways in which we interact with one another and, consequently, investigates how the objects that surround us play an active role in our relationships—they are never innocent or neutral.

I take my cue from the films of Charlie Chaplin and Buster Keaton, and try to be humorously critical of architectural conditions through architecture itself: exaggerating certain codes of behavior, playing tricks on one's expectations, and breaking certain rules in order to generate alternative modes of interaction. I am interested in the body as a point of departure and in the magic of the everyday. My "tools for everyday living" expose the idiosyncrasies of interactions that tend to pass unnoticed. At times I intentionally leave some of the tools incomplete or inconclusive to provoke users to adapt, adjust, and perhaps misuse them. I see my work as latent potential—intimate prosthetics waiting for users to appropriate and implement them into their everyday life.

Public Support
Can public facades become truly public?

In order to convert public facades into spaces of habitation, a series of bumps are stuck to facades where no urban furniture exists. As a result, what used to be a blank facade transforms into a comfortable surface to lean on. The shape and height of the bumps insinuate possible positions for the body to take while waiting for the bus or a friend.

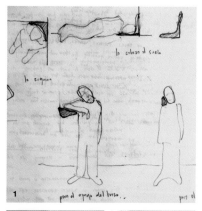

1: Sketches of possible positions
2: Shapes of bumps
3: An elbow rest
4: A back rest 5: A head rest

The Segregator
Are limits arbitrarily defined?

A critical response to the ever-increasing presence of security gates, the Segregator exaggerates the mechanism of the average security gate to an extreme in order to ridicule the perception of authority. The Segregator consists of a black-and-yellow pivotable needle attached to a seat, where—in the spirit of Charlie Chaplin movies, where body movements are critical tools—one must sit on the seat in order to lift the needle. The seat is placed a bit higher than a typical chair, requiring a series of uncomfortable movements to reach it. This indirectly ridicules "authority" by making the very action necessary to exercise their power seem absurd.

The Segregator was put into practice in different arbitrary spots around the city—places where no restriction was necessary. A group of students asked drivers passing by generic security questions: "Where are you heading?" "Who are you visiting?" "What is the purpose of your visit?" To our surprise people did not question the absurdity of our structure and passively "collaborated" with us in the enforcement of random and ridiculous limits.

Designed in collaboration with students of Universidad Iberoamericana

1: A security barrier lifts when someone sits on the chair
2: Authority subjected to ridicule through an absurd movement
3: The Segregator at work in different parts of the city

Birdhouses
What is the minimal architectural gesture needed to encourage appropriation?

Birdhouses consists of intentionally unfinished structures mounted on trees in a neglected zone of Chapultepec Park in Mexico City. The inclusion of only the minimal amount of physical elements required for habitation allows the user to modify and adapt these structures as necessary. The open structures function as birdhouses in that birdhouses are typically used by different species during different seasons, allowing varied users to change, add, and affect the structure as it becomes necessary. The Birdhouses is, therefore, a framework that registers the varied users as they use the structures.

Designed in collaboration with students of Universidad Iberoamericana.

1: Sketch of a minimal gesture implying habitation
2: An open frame awaiting users to adapt it to their needs
3: An oversized traditional birdhouse sized for humans
4: A roof and floor barely suggested

Unstable Obstacle
Can a structure become more stable as more people use it?

A rocking structure in the shape of a small boat offers an alternative to public benches. The Unstable Obstacle encourages cooperation—the more people participate, the more stable it becomes. However, this stability relies on the establishment of a dialogue between users. The second person to sit on the Unstable Obstacle must respond to where the first person is sitting; otherwise, the structure flips. The unstable structure is a mechanism that promotes collective participation through physical dialogue.

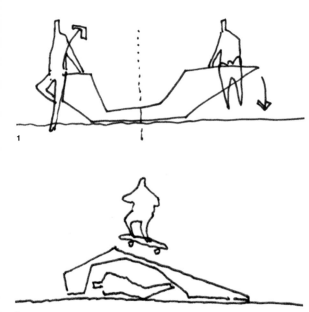

1

2

1: Sketch of structure showing the balance required between users
2: Sketch of structure flipped upside down for use as a shelter or a skateboard ramp
3: One user 4: Two users
5: Three users 6: The structure as a refuge

Urban Oasis
Can the presence of another user in a public space enrich one's experience of it?

Intended to promote interaction between strangers sharing the same public space, the Urban Oasis is an alternative proposal for urban furniture where the presence of users affects its composition. A system of pulleys connects elevated seats to buckets filled with flowering plants laying on the floor; as each person sits on a specific seat, he or she acts as a counterweight to the bucket and lifts it up. Each seat is connected to one or two buckets positioned near the other seats; as a result, a bucket that was initially at ground level is lifted to the height of a sitting person so that one can smell the flowers. In this way, the presence of one user affects the atmosphere of another user. The Urban Oasis becomes a space where the presence of other people is desirable.

The structure was assembled during the Lisbon Architecture Triennale, in a park where homeless people sleep. During construction, they became interested in the structure and ended up helping contruct and taking care of it.

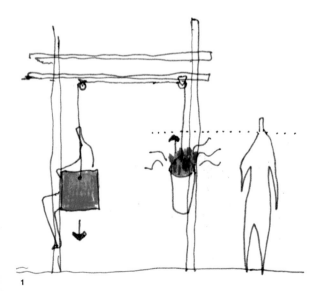

1

1: Sketch of structure
2: Collage of structure

2

3: Structure mounted at a neglected park in Lisbon during the Lisbon Architecture Triennale

4: Homeless people who slept in the park, becoming involved with the construction of Urban Oasis
5: Homeless people taking care of the plants

Information Center
Can a simple volume generate a complex experience?

Designed as a meeting and information space for the Plataforma Art Festival
in Puebla, Mexico, the Information Center is a simple volume threaded with white
plastic that, from a distance, appears solid. Yet, as one approaches the volume,
one discovers its permeability to the light, sounds, and smells filtering from the
Zocalo plaza. The interior space is organized by an undulating wooden floor that
generates a work table, a reading area, and hammocks positioned over planters
set into the floor. At the far end of the volume, a fully mirrored wall expands
the perceived space.

Designed in collaboration with Mauricio Rocha

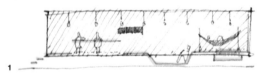

1

2

1: Sketch of interior functions
2: The simple white volume contrasts with the local baroque architecture
3: Interior reading and resting places with diffused light

Public Mobile Library
Must a library always be an interior room where one sits on a chair to read?

The Public Mobile Library is a proposal for an itinerant reading space composed of a simple cube. Three of the cube's faces are made of woven white plastic strips designed to diffuse light as it enters the interior space. One of the nonwoven facades is a wooden bookshelf that faces the interior, whose exterior wooden surface is left blank in order to allow posters and other information to be glued to it. The opposite face is a pivoting structure—hinged at the bottom—that opens up the cube to the public. The multiple levels of the pivoting structure allow it not only to be used as an entryway stair but also as a sitting and laying area. The Public Mobile Library is built on wheels so it can travel to different public areas around the city.

Designed in collaboration with Mauricio Rocha

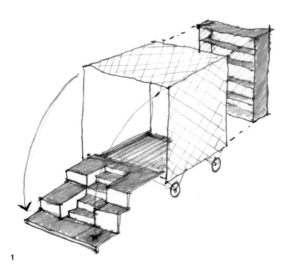

1

1: Sketch of composition
2: Library closed 3: Library open
4: Profile view of open library

Reading Room
Can architecture make a welcoming gesture?

Set inside what used to be a neglected, unused room adjacent to a small patio leading to the Museum of Contemporary Art in Puebla, Mexico, the Reading Room provides a resting space for museum-goers as well as for the many people passing by toward a nearby park. In order to attract users and to make an architecturally welcoming gesture, a long table on wheels can be pulled out onto the patio. A series of hammock-swings are positioned randomly throughout the rest of the space—generating a playful and cozy reading room.

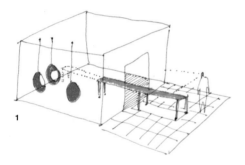

1

2

1: Sketch of spatial connection with patio
2: Swings randomly positioned inside
3: Table on wheels projected into patio

Scaffolding Room
Can an architectural element help the occupants share a single space?

In a room shared by two children, where each sleeps in one of the mezzanines located at opposite sides of the room, a strategically placed movable staircase permits access to either of the two mezzanines. Different spatial conditions in the room's main space are created depending on where the stair is positioned: one arrangement separates the room into two equal areas, while the other leaves most of the space open. In either configuration the firemen's pole allow the children to come down from the mezzanines without the stair. The unused handrails have potential to be used in a playful manner, as structures from where to hang toys or swing oneself around. The room becomes a scaffolding structure—a framework awaiting the kids to appropriate, adapt, and transform it with their changing needs.

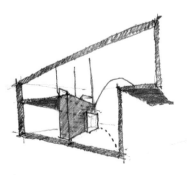 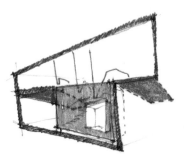

1

1: Sketch of staircase in its two positions
2: Staircase positioned toward first mezzanine, leaving the main area open
3: Staircase positioned toward second mezzanine, dividing the room in two

2

3

Collector's Studio
Can an architectural composition generate a narrative?

As part of a studio remodeling, the client—an art collector—needed a bookshelf. While clearing the space of old furniture, I noticed a room full of abandoned crates, once used to store pieces of art. This led me to propose that the bookshelf be an ad hoc assemblage using and adapting the crates. The juxtaposition of each stamp, mark, signature, or logo that remained on the crates contributed to the construction of a collaged narrative—an informal biography of the accidents, voyages, and experiences that the client has undergone since he began collecting art.

1

2

1: Sketch showing the accumulation inherent in collecting
2: General composition of bookshelf
3: Detail of marks, stamps, and logos on crates
4: Doors and chairs were also generated out of crates

Sliding Table
Can a piece of furniture elicit friction?

Based on the number game where a void allows each number to strategically move into the void in order to position itself into sequence, the Sliding Table consists of eight solid, sliding modules—each with a specific function and treatment—and one empty module arranged on a three-by-three grid. The empty module allows the user to move each solid module to a different position one movement at a time. As a result, rather than asking for the bottle of wine on the table, one can move the module holding the bottle of wine closer—perhaps generating a certain friction in the process with another person sitting nearby.

1: Sketch showing the awkwardness of asking for a saltshaker
2: Collage of interaction
3: Sequence of shifting-module positions

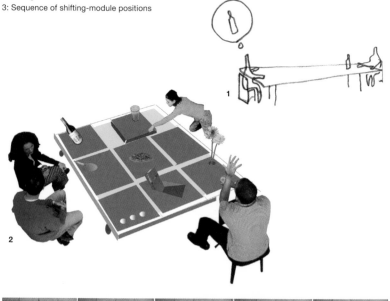

Seesaw Table
Can a table affect the way we interact?

During a meal shared by two people, one person usually dominates the conversation, leaving the other person to eat quietly. The Seesaw Table subverts that dynamic and balances the conditions of interaction. In order to be close enough to eat food set on the table, a person must be in the up position on the seesaw; therefore, the individual in the down position of the seesaw is far from the food, and can talk while the other is eating. The oscillation between the positions makes the conversation a balancing act.

1: Sketch showing the unbalanced interaction between two people eating
2: Drawing of mechanism
3: A seesaw-inspired table balances the interaction between two people

Mexican Army Shelf
Can a piece of furniture be as versatile as a Swiss army knife?

Inspired by the Swiss army knife, the Mexican Army Shelf houses a number of individual shelves, each designed for a specific use. Most of the uses are generated by needs that arise as one is walking in or out of the house: there is a shelf to store the mail, a shelf to store different sized coins, one to write messages on (with pencil and Post-it integrated into it), a shelf to hang a coat, a shelf to hang sets of keys, and a shelf with a mirror incorporated into it to look at oneself before stepping out. The shelves are hinged at one of their two ends like blades in a Swiss army knife and can be pulled out or retracted as necessary.

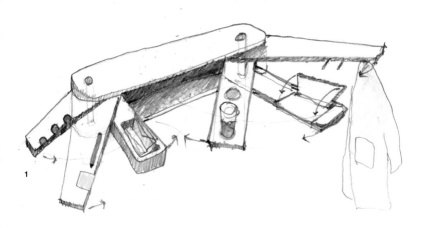

1

1: Sketch of the shelf's different functions
2: Sequence of individual shelves being pulled out

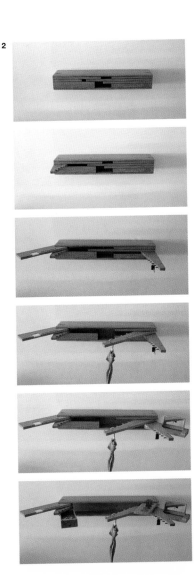

PRODUCTORA

48 Granados House

50 Call Center Churubusco II

52 Mixcoac House

54 Expo Francis Alys

56 Musso House

58 House in Virreyes

60 C.S.I. Corporate Headquarters

62 Museum of Contemporary Art, Lima (LiMac)

66 Tsunami Memorial Site Competition

68 Installation for Iñaki Bonillas

70 Hotel Tulum

Paul Feyerabend's epistemological masterpiece, *Against Method*, was first published as an essay in 1970; as the title suggests, it is a criticism of the idea that science has only a single method to expand the scope of knowledge. Feyerabend describes the history of science as a complex fabric of serendipity, poetic challenges, erroneous observations, and hazardous discoveries in a continuous dialectic with rational and scientific procedures. Contradiction and irrationality are, therefore, just as much a part of a strategy as the established scientific roads to enlightenment, and are particularly important in the challenging of fundamental assumptions that lead to revolutions or paradigm shifts.

We draw the same conclusions in the field of architecture. Our architectural projects always start with an anarchic series of intuitive explorations. Sometimes they are linked to specific environmental parameters, budget limitations, or programmatic necessities; in other occasions they are mere formal explorations accomplished through drawings or models. There is no way to judge the supremacy of one method over the other—the only way to discover the value of initial intuition is by developing the project, to make headway. When a strong diagram loses its power during the course of a project, perhaps the initial axioms were wrong. When, on the contrary, the conceptual idea becomes stronger, and we begin to perceive a correspondence between the starting point and the resulting solutions (technical, structural, architectonic), we can call the project "proven."

Granados House
Chihuahua, Mexico, 2006 (under construction)

The Granados House is part of a golf club community in the desertlike northern region of Mexico. The dwelling was designed to accommodate the special climatic circumstances of the area: in winter temperatures can fall to 14°F, while in summertime temperatures can rise to above 104°F. The differences between daytime and nighttime temperatures can vary by as much as twenty degrees. To balance the extreme temperature differences, we partially buried the house into the mountain slope to take advantage of the soil's thermal mass. The colder soil around the house absorbs heat accumulated during the day, and at night the ground gives off heat to the building. The house is organized around a series of patios and roof openings that provide light, ventilation, and views to different areas of the house. The sloped roof acts as a new topography, which blurs the boundaries between the constructed area and the surrounding landscape.

1: Rendering of exterior
2–9: Construction site, May 2007

Call Center Churubusco II
Mexico City, 2007

This project consists of a low-budget call center in an industrialized area in southern Mexico City. Although the construction method and materials used are typical for the area—a simple modular steel frame as structure and profiled metal sheets for the volume's facade—the Call Center Churubusco II evokes elegance. To provide abundant natural light, we removed large vertical strips from the modular metal sheeting, creating an equal open-and-closed distribution to the facade. The open segments paint striped patterns of sunlight onto the work floor of the interior. Special detailing of the entrance doors continues the simple logic of positive-negative along the center's entire perimeter. The long vertical openings along the facade lend the volume a certain classical beauty—the typical industrial box transformed into an elegant, translucent curtain.

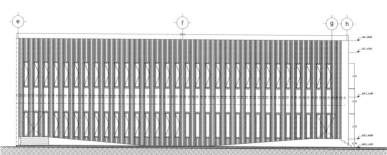

1

1: Main-facade elevation
2: Exterior view, under construction
3: Interior view, under construction

Mixcoac House
Mexico City, 2007
In collaboration with Frente/Juan Pablo Maza

This project for a small house in a middle-class neighborhood of Mexico City is a play on scale and perspective. The limited area of the site inspired us to maximize the perceived experience of the space.

The ground-floor plan was divided lengthwise into an indoor living area and a garden that extends along the whole depth of the site. The incline of the garden (ascending toward the back) and the gradually narrowing modulation of the living-area windows makes the garden appear deeper than it really is. The upper-floor volume shifts horizontally, breaking the orthogonality of the scheme and creating an overhang that shades the garden. The ground level of the small house includes the kitchen, studio, living area, bathroom, and a bedroom; the upper floor contains the master bedroom, walk-in closet, bathroom, and terrace. The total floor area of the house comprises little more than nine hundred square feet (ninety square meters).

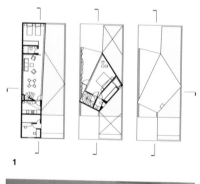

1

2

3

4

1: Floor plans 2: View from above (Photo: Juan Pablo Maza)
3: Elliptical staircase (Photo: Juan Pablo Maza)
4: View from street level with the original facade (Photo: Juan Pablo Maza)
5: View toward garden from entrance of the house (Photo: Paul Czitrom)

Expo Francis Alÿs
Mexico City, 2006

The Belgian artist Francis Alÿs asked us to support him in the design of his exhibition at the Colegio de San Ildefonso, in the historical center of Mexico City. His proposal included the placement of a platform in the huge chapel to divide the existing space into smaller compartments. Inspired by some of the spatial qualities of the Danteum (1938) by Giuseppe Terragni, we multiplied the number of supporting columns and reduced their dimensions as much as possible. Diagonal beams, introduced to give the structure horizontal stability, transformed the rigid grid of columns into a mysterious and complex forest of lines, which allude to Alÿs's contemplative walks through the chaotic neighborhoods of Mexico City.

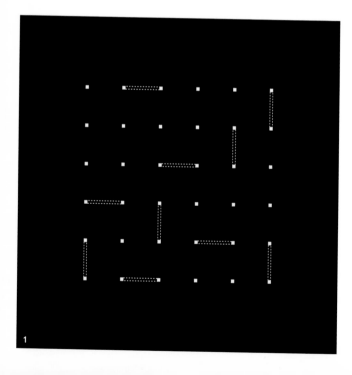

1

1: Schematic ground-floor plan—columns and diagonal beams for horizontal stability
2–4: Exhibition at the Colegio de San Ildefonso (Photos: Cyril Rozent)

Musso House
Puerto Escondido, Mexico, 2007 (under construction)

Mexico has enormous climatic diversity—working in different areas of the country requires knowledge of local and traditional building systems to respond to variations in temperature and humidity. Musso House is a summerhouse located on the coast of the Oaxaca State. The buildings of this region are usually topped with a palapa roof—a steep structure of wooden beams covered with several layers of palm leaves. The house is a simple, autonomous, triangular volume parallel to the seashore. The house's only alteration to the typical palapa roof is a large cut at the land side, where the main entry is located. Here the garden that surrounds the house extends into the more public areas of the house, separating them from the private ones. The perforations of the two walls that flank the entry provide filtered light and ventilation to the dining area and the night hall, which connects the bedrooms and bathrooms. The twisting of the roof at the seaside provides protection for the bedrooms and opens up the views from the living area toward the ocean.

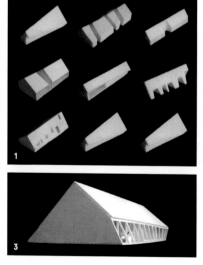

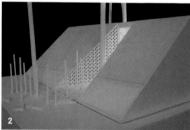

1: First study models 2: Model of the cut at the land side of the volume
3. Study model of the twisted facade, facing seaside 4: Wooden triangular framework
5: Access to the house 6: View from the seaside

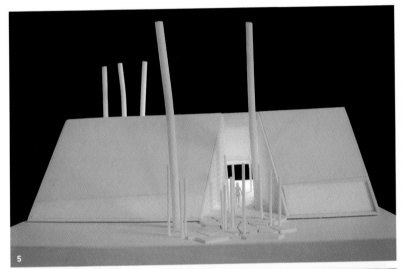

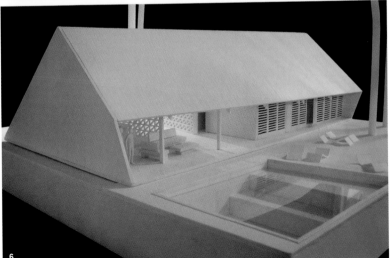

House in Virreyes
Lomas Virreyes, Mexico City, 2006

Clients are a key factor in the development of projects. For the refurbishment of a seventies-era villa in a residential area of Mexico City, our clients proposed that we test and rethink daily domestic routines such as bathing, dining, or watching television.

A part of the renovation of the entire house was the development of a bathroom that would avoid commonplace elements such as tiles, mirrors, and typical bathroom furniture. The resulting design consists of two converging, moveable wooden walls—an abstract, complementary space next to the bedroom. The sliding and opening of these wooden panels alters the bathroom's use—making it either a sauna or a shower area or allowing access to the toilet or washbasin.

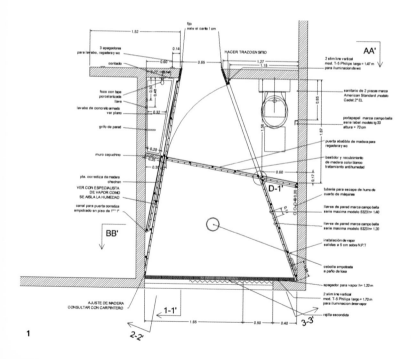

1: Floor plan
2: View from inside bathroom toward hall of the bedroom (Photo: Paul Czitrom)

C.S.I. Corporate Headquarters
Mexico City, 2006 (under construction)

The new corporate offices for the C.S.I. Group are situated on a deep site along Avenida Revolución, one of the most important avenues of Mexico City. The client requested a considerable space for the production area and a large office space visible from the avenue. To diminish the impact to the neighborhood, we divided the structure into three interconnected volumes: a lower volume housing the call center and two slim towers housing the offices. The highest tower has eleven floors and faces north, toward Chapultepec Park. The lower tower in the back of the site has seven floors and is orientated toward the avenue, engaging in a sculptural interaction with the other tower. The horizontal volume is organized along a deep interior patio directly connected with the street. This semipublic area is the heart of the building and distributes the flow of people toward their corresponding parts of the complex. It also contains the employees' lunch area, a cafeteria with terrace, and a small commercial area.

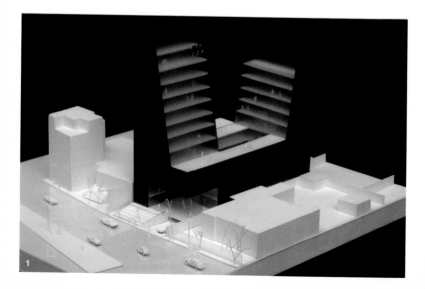

1

1: Model
2: Volumetric study models

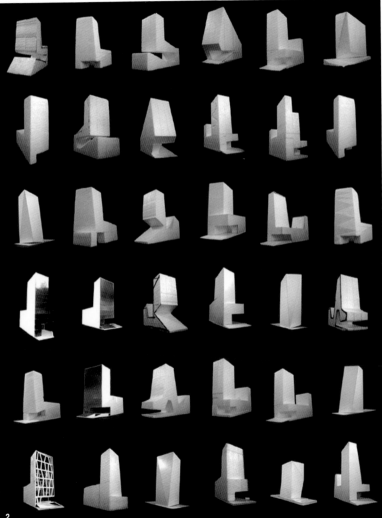

2

Museum of Contemporary Art, Lima (LiMac)
Lima, Peru, 2006

The project for the LiMac combines two distinct museum typologies: the nineteenth-century museum, which consists of a succession of rectangular rooms (the classical exhibition space), and the museum space of the twentieth century, the white, open space of the loft or gallery (the free floor plan with columns). A gradation of volumes in the central area of the LiMac is developed as a series of columns on a free floor plan at one side of the space, and an exhibition hall converted into a group of square rooms divided by corridors on the other side. As a result, the museum space creates an ambiguous relationship between the contained exhibition "rooms" and the open space that flows in between the volumes. A perimeter of auxiliary spaces is organized around this central exhibition space and is illuminated and ventilated through vast green patios cut out of the landscape.

LiMac is an invisible museum. The international impact of expressive, daring, and loud museums—like Frank Gehry's Guggenheim Museum in Bilbao, Spain, or Zaha Hadid's museum in Wolfsburg, Germany—made us question this evolution in contemporary museum architecture. The idea of building a museum hidden in the desert's topography offered an attractive alternative. We thought of a building without facade or silhouette—a building absorbed by the landscape—hiding a mysterious space inside, almost like an Egyptian tomb. We imagined a labyrinthine space lit by patios and roof lights, perceivable only as a series of excavations or triangular surfaces breaking the existing topography—an abstract composition in the Peruvian landscape. Organized almost exclusively on one level to eliminate costs for personal and freight elevators, the museum also minimizes the use of air conditioning through its underground placement, where temperature and humidity levels are far more balanced then in the open desert of Peru.

Finally, this museum represents an ambition. It not only expresses our belief in the necessity for a center for contemporary art in a metropolis such as Lima, but it also communicates our desire to build an architecture of spatial mystery and delight. An architecture that refers to forgotten pasts, generates new experiences, and leaves—like a Nazca drawing—a trace in the desert. It is a manifestation of contemporary culture and architecture in the landscape of Peru.

1: Study models, interiors, and roofscapes

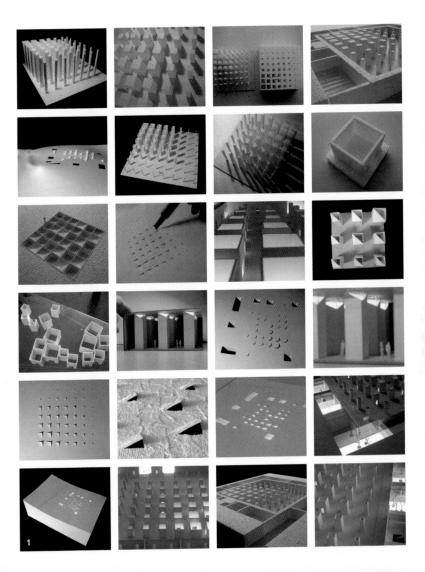

2: Site plan

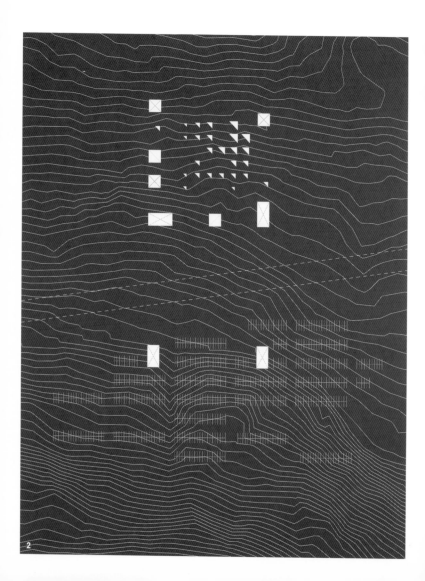

3: Rendering of triangular roof lights in a desert landscape
4: Model of interior spaces

Tsunami Memorial Site Competition
Oslo, Norway, 2006

NATURE: When we observe nature over time, we perceive how fragile and blurry the limits between its different elements are—life and death, solid and air, sea and land seem to coexist in an ever-evolving landscape. The history of nature is the tale of invisible metamorphoses and spectacular incidents in a scenography without curtains. Nature evolves without conscience. It is there.

CULTURE: A human creation incited by the idea of reason, culture gives meaning to natural order: to draw a rectangle in the sand to delimit what is yours. The inside defines cultivated space; the outside, nature. This superimposition of culture onto nature has always been a ferocious conquest of the other; the result is an unstable equilibrium between opposites. The geography questions nature, frames the known world, and classifies it with landscapes and territories. A drawing of the mapa mundi.

DISASTER: In the pure context of nature, disaster does not exist—it is called change. Disaster is a cultural appellation for the natural phenomenon of abrupt change. When natural disasters occur, the balance between nature and culture is shocked abruptly. These events provoke thought and reactivate our conscience about nature.

MEMORY: Nature does not have memory. It does not recognize guilt. It exists outside of any historical order. The introduction of a monument into an environment forces the natural context into the logic of historical space and time. The monument is one of the strongest cultural tokens in the field of symbols—it leaves a trace of our existence and disguises our fear of disappearing.

PROJECT: To commemorate the victims of the Tsunami disaster of 2004, we felt obliged to focus not on personal loss and grief, but rather on the fragile relationship between culture and nature, between Cartesian space and the entropic unknown. The insertion of a perfect square into the site—trapped between the sea and land—offers a chance for reflection on the dialectics between man and nature. Situated between low and high sea levels, the square can become an extension of land toward the sea, or be "taken" by the sea and almost disappear.

1: Model
2–5: Collage studies of interaction between sea and shore
(mounted black-and-white photocopies)

Installation for Iñaki Bonillas
OMR Gallery, Mexico City, 2007

Iñaki Bonillas asked for architectural support for his site-specific installation
Naufragio con espectador (Shipwreck with Spectator) in the OMR Gallery in
Mexico City. His piece plays with the obvious tilt of both the floors and walls of
the gallery building: four platforms create the illusion of a sea of light that viewers
can submerge themselves in or walk on, shaping a new possibility for perception
of the gallery's space. Four steel frames, leveled by a system of metal bolts, were
introduced into the gallery space. The platforms were then covered with MDF
(medium density fiberboard) panels and airbrushed in situ with white epoxy-
polymer paint for a smooth surface. Underneath these platforms a series of cold
neon lights were installed to cast baseboards of light onto the gallery walls,
emphasizing the height difference between the balanced platforms and the
inclined floor.

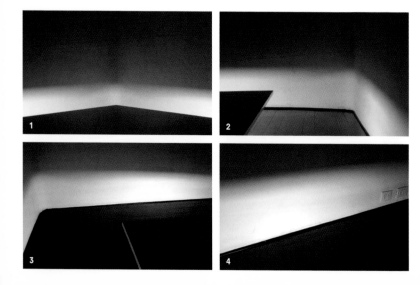

1–4: Details of the light from beneath the platforms illuminating the gallery space
5: Overall view of the gallery space with leveled platforms

5

Hotel Tulum
Quintana Roo, Mexico, 2007 (under construction)

Hotel Tulum's site is a plot of land compressed between a coastal highway and rocky seashore in a beautiful area in the south of Mexico, next to ancient Mayan pyramids. The project is designed as a system of positive-negative volumes that frames the different interesting views around the site: views toward the sea, toward the vegetation, and upward to the sky.

The hotel's rectangular volumes, arranged in the existing landscape, include a central building and ten individual volumes for guests. The main volume separates the highway from the rest of the site and forms a long landmark along the road. The individual room-volumes all contain indoor and outdoor areas situated above, below, or beside the actual room. These spaces serve as enclosed private patios or shaded terraces. There is no electricity for the site, and the small hotel generates its own energy by solar and wind systems. Opening up opposite sides of each volume generates a continuous cross ventilation through the spaces and eliminates the need for air conditioning.

1: View of the existing landscape 2: Study models of the rectangular volumes
3: Model of main volume next to the coastal highway
4: Model of entire site from road to seaside

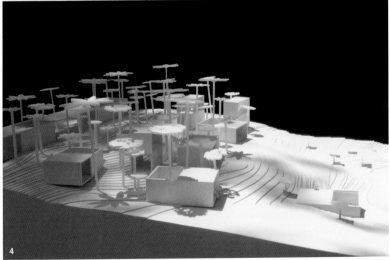

PARA

74 **Rorschach Test**

78 **Mobile Art Park**

84 **'Lifting Mies**

88 **Macri Park**

94 **Times Square Military Lifestyle Center**

PARA Is a Prefix.

"Para" can mean beside, with, and alongside; or against, counter, outside, and beyond.

Working as a prefix, PARA attaches itself to familiar organizations to produce foreign results:

Paradox, Paranormal, Parable, Parabolic, Paradiddle, Paradigm, Paradisaic, Paradise, Paragon, Paralanguage, Paralegal, Parallax, Parallel, Paralogism, Paralysis, Paramedic, Parameter, Paramilitary, Paramount, Paranoia, Paraphernalia, Parasite, Paratactic...

PARA Bullshits.*

The Bullshitter is not concerned with truth or falsity. Rather, Bullshitting uses uncertainty to table alternative propositions, convincing fictions, or elliptical logics. The process of Bullshitting is contentious and unsettling. The Bullshitter is not a liar, what he says may very well be true...

PARA Likes Loopholes.

The loophole is a model of opportunistic deviance. Like lawyers exploiting contract ambiguities, financiers engaging in arbitrage, or accountants seeking tax shelters, the loophole is an opening for the dexterous professional.

*The bullshit reference is from Harry Frankfurt, *On Bullshit* (Princeton, NJ: Princeton University Press, 2005).

Rorschach Test
1,000 Postcards Competition, 2006

The Rorschach test is a proof. It is a method of psychological evaluation—not so much for seeking objective meaning, but more for interpreting the psychosis of the patient. The inkblot is neither formal nor formless. It is a formless form, so empty of inherent meaning that it is brimming with potential content. It is a shape that acquires significance according to how it is perceived or used. Can "empty formalism" actually make more meaningful architecture? We used the Rorschach test as a device to evaluate "inherited" predicaments within the discipline of architecture. It works as a loophole into architecture's "psyche" by questioning modes of practice, techniques of production, codes of values, and public perceptions.

    While architecture's relevance relies on the recognition of what is familiar, architecture's survival relies on what will always be foreign. The Rorschach straddles this line between familiar and foreign—it is often both recognizable and indistinguishable.

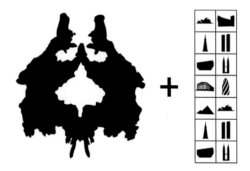

1

1: Diagram
2: Rorschach Test mirror installation

3: Rorschach postcard
4: Geography test

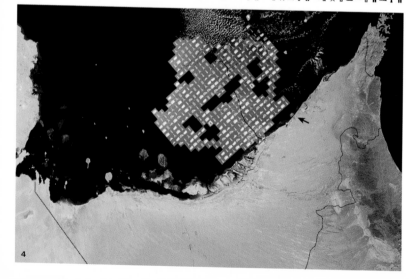

3

4

5: Currency test
6: Diagram 7: Marketing test
8: History test

5

7

6

Plans of Versailles and Paris in 1789.

8

Mobile Art Park
Roosevelt Island, New York, 2005

The Roosevelt Island Mobile Art Park is conceived as a network of floating barges. Inheriting Southpoint Park's history as a landfill, the barges gather together to form a vibrant community of artists and art enthusiasts. The barges link to each other in various combinations and form a migrating network that extends throughout the regional waters of New York's five boroughs and beyond. They combine to accommodate different events, from an art biennale to a skateboarding competition. Moving around the city, the barges bridge vibrant, culturally disparate enclave communities of artists already thriving in the city.

The Mobile Art Park floats ambiguously between Nature—embodied by Southpoint Park—and Culture. Each two-story barge is composed of two general programs: leisure space—garden, cafe, skate park, etc.—on the upper level and art space on the lower level. Like a naval fleet composed of different ships, the barges can be deployed in various programmatic combinations to suit their destination; through these relationships the production and consumption of art is mixed with everyday leisure activities. The Mobile Art Park addresses the issue of accessibility as cultural inclusion and maximizes access to the world of art, facilitating the incorporation of art into everyday life.

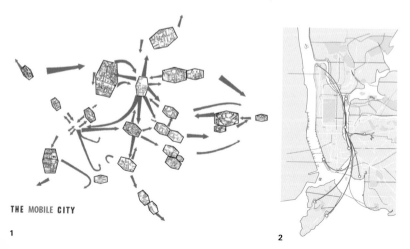

THE MOBILE CITY

1

2

1: Diagram 2: Circulation diagram
3: Program scenarios
4: Plan

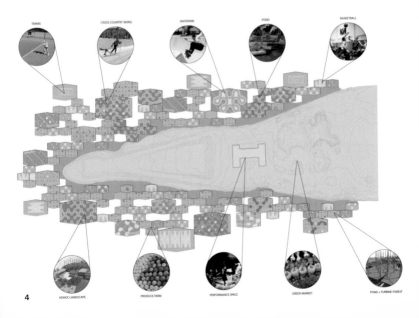

TENNIS · CROSS COUNTRY SKIING · SKATEPARK · POND · BASKETBALL

ADHOC LANDSCAPE · PRODUCE FARM · PERFORMANCE SPACE · GREEN MARKET · POND + TURBINE FOREST

5: Landscape-program matrix 6: Axonometric of large barge
7: Axonometric of medium barge 8: Axonometric of small barge

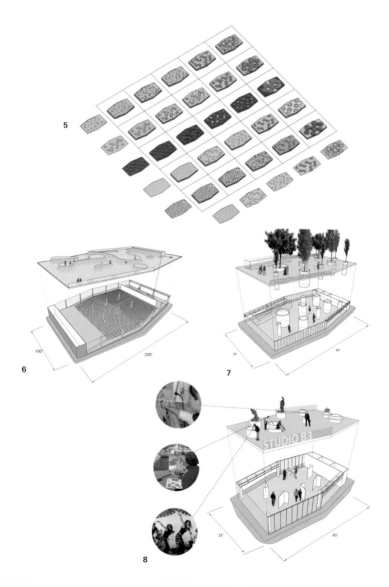

9: Occupancy diagram 10: Program scenarios
11: Acrylic model

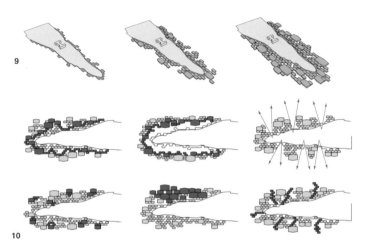

9

10

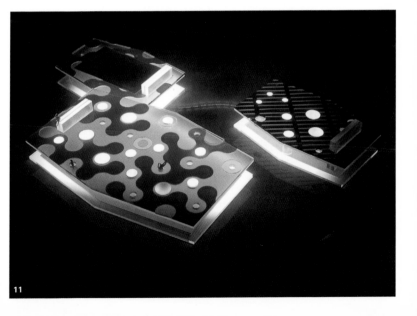

11

12–15: Renderings

'Lifting Mies
Seagram Building, New York, New York, 2005

It is said that architecture reacts to culture too slowly. Perhaps the lagging profession might learn something from the swift, identity-transforming procedures of plastic surgery.

Mies van der Rohe's Seagram Building—the epitome of late modernism's embrace of Fordist repetition, built in 1958—is the subject of our case study. Could a strategy of modification—a post-Fordist nip-and-tuck—rejuvenate this aging trophy to let it stand alongside Manhattan's newest starlet towers? 'Lifting Mies is a catalog of surgical procedures that would operate directly on Mies's canonical decorative I-beams. The case study's technique eschews the addition of unnecessary material—the conventional approach to ornamentation—and instead relies on the alteration of what already exists, as a facelift would. The surgery makes ornamentation inconspicuous, just as a successful facelift transforms one's identity without revealing the work of the surgeon. By cutting, reshaping, and stitching, surgical techniques transform ornamentation into an essential part of the body.

1, 2: Facelift
3: Elevation (A), modifications, modification details
4: Elevation (B), modifications, modification details

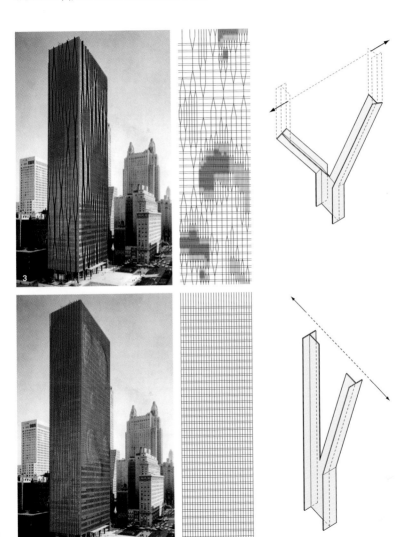

4: Elevation (C), modifications, modification details
5: Elevation (D), modifications, modification details

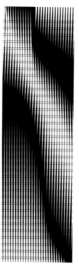

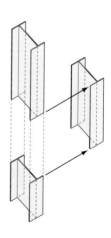

6: Elevation (E), modifications, modification details

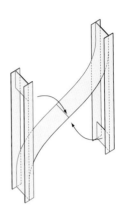

Macri Park
Brooklyn, New York, 2007

There are two types of parks: public and private. Macri Park, a 1,250-square-foot bar with an open loop of public circulation running through its private space, combines the two types into one. Large custom-made glass doors are recessed into the walls in order to further the breezeway character of the space. A small rear yard connects the outdoor and indoor zones through a concrete floorplate that runs continuously from interior to exterior. Luminaries inset into the ground are distributed throughout the interior and exterior spaces to further emphasize continuity. And a twisted, dropped ceiling augments the existing low ceiling, making room for mechanical equipment yet also reading as a seamless connection between the two exterior spaces.

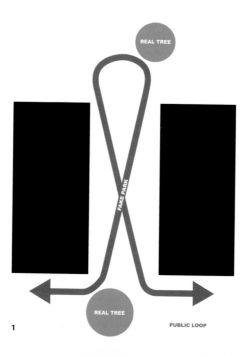

1

1: Diagram
2: View into back garden (Photo: © Frank Oudeman 2007)
3: Back garden under construction

4: Floor plan

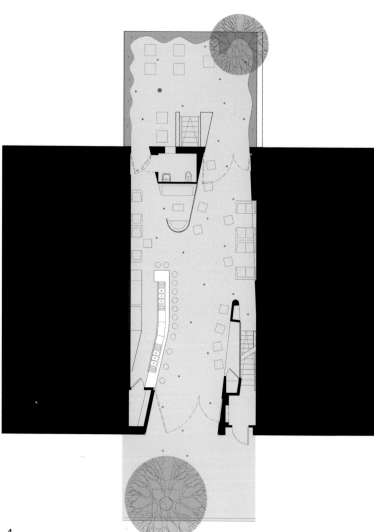

5: Section
6: View to sidewalk (Photo: © Frank Oudeman 2007)

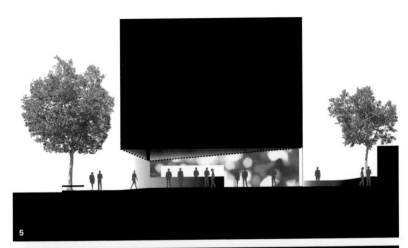

7: Exploded axonmetric

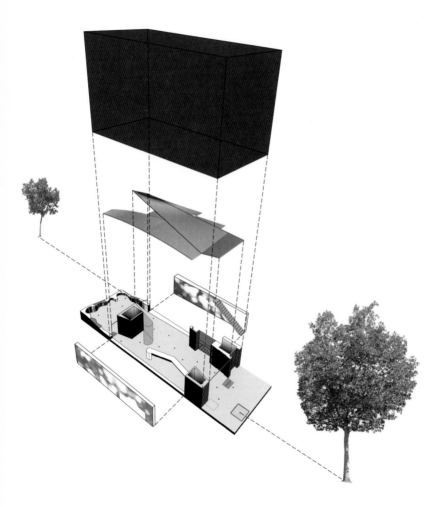

8: View from back garden (Photo: © Frank Oudeman 2007)

Times Square Military Lifestyle Center
New York, New York, 2006

In 2006 we were approached by the U.S. Department of Defense to propose an alternative to the existing recruiting station in Times Square. The predicament was one of identity: The military wanted to re-present itself in a new light. How could architecture help the American public readily relate to the military?

The proposal recasts the opaque nature of the typical military-industrial complex—epitomized by the Pentagon—as a potential source of entertainment to visually and programmatically align the center with its Times Square context. The U.S. Military budget for the development of new technologies in 2006 was 147 billion dollars. (Surely this technology was not developed only for imperialism and war.) The Times Square Military Lifestyle Center mines this cache of new technologies with a domestic agenda: to make the military's identity accessible to the public in the forms of entertainment, sport, and a new military lifestyle.

The Pentagon is transplanted to Times Square as an icon from which a new image of the military can be constructed. The mass of the Pentagon is lifted, cloudlike, from the ground, allowing the street and the public into its courtyard. Clad in highly reflective inflated-ETFE cushions, the floating cloud is camouflaged by its context, reflecting at various points either the purity of the sky or the chaotic street life of Times Square.

The proposed recruiting station engages the public through two core American values: consumerism and entertainment. The Military Lifestyle Center provides many familiar amenities—including health and fitness, a space for socializing, and a theater—yet these spaces are uniquely enabled by demilitarized technologies that have been made available to the public—a gesture toward domesticating military life.

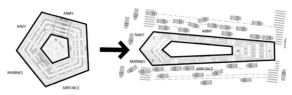

1   WASHINGTON, D.C.   TIMES SQUARE, NEW YORK

1: Conceptual diagram
2: Rendering

2

3: Domesticating technology

TECHNOLOGY BRIDGES THE MILITARY-TECHNOLOGY DIVIDE

MILITARY TECHNOLOGY

DOMESTICATED PROGRAM

SIMULATORS → **GAMING ARCADE**

Developed to train pilots as infantry men, simulation technology has the potential to train even the youngest American for the battle of life.

NON-LETHAL HEAT GUN → **DO ASK DON'T TELL DAY SPA**

A non-lethal weapon that is capable of heating the skin to 140 deg. F. Infared technology could be adapted for use in saunas or other intimate settings.

AAS STEROIDS → **ROTC FITNESS GYM**

Anabolic steriods have long been developed by the military for use in body-building. If intergrated into a healthy diet, they could benefit the health and well-being of all Americans.

PHEROMONES → **CLUB USO**

Developed to break up riotous crowds, doses of gaseous pheromones drive people to the brink of insanity with sexual appetite — an ideal addition to New York's next hottest club.

PROPAGANDA → **MOVIE THEATER**

Military-sponsored films that invoke patriotic emotions have long penetrated the American psyche, but never before has a theater been dedicated soley to propoganda films.

INFLATABLE STRUCTURES → **BEACH CABANA**

Inflatable air structures used for military encampemnts are deployed as cabanas for the urban beach deck—temporary shelter from the blazing sun and neon lights.

4: Section
5: Collage

4

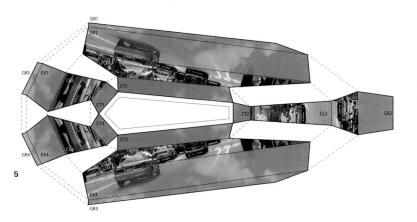

5

6: Unfolded surface

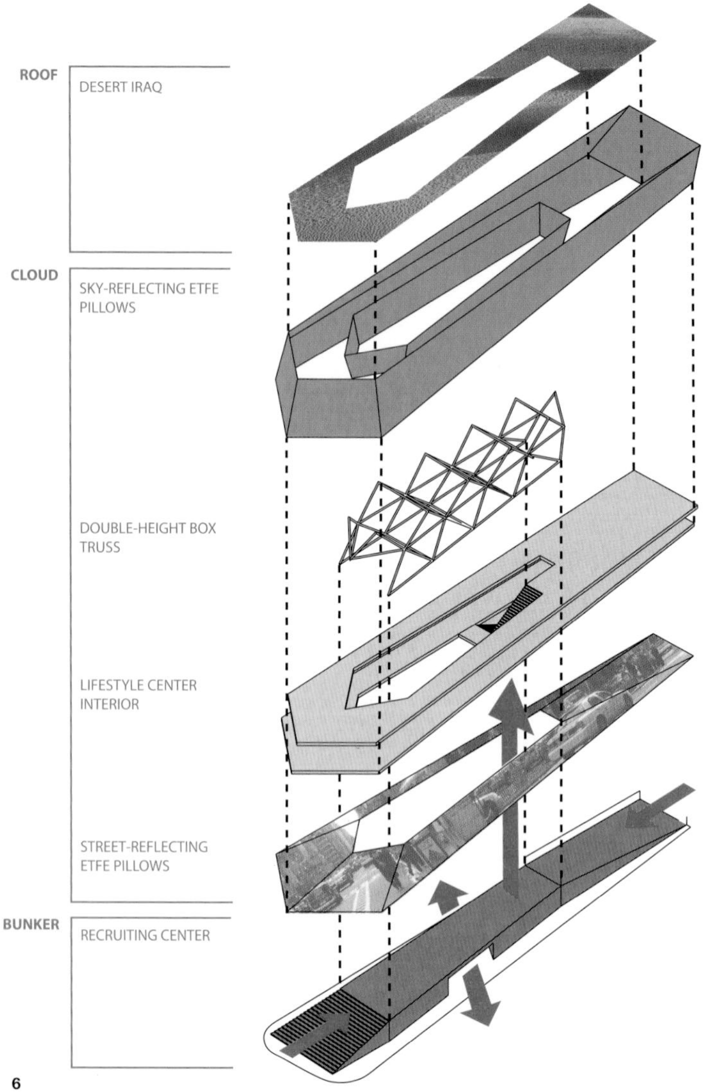

ROOF — DESERT IRAQ

CLOUD — SKY-REFLECTING ETFE PILLOWS

DOUBLE-HEIGHT BOX TRUSS

LIFESTYLE CENTER INTERIOR

STREET-REFLECTING ETFE PILLOWS

BUNKER — RECRUITING CENTER

6

7: Model
8: Rendering

Jinhee Park

102 Czech National Library
106 HBNY (Parenthetical Space)
110 Soft Lofts
112 Big Dig Building
118 Asian Cultural Complex
122 Boston Harbor Pavilion
124 Sponge Park

When the singularity of truth has been replaced by the multiplicity of diversity, the meaning of "proof" also shifts. Instead of a simple stacking of evidence where one theorem is built upon another, proof has become a constellation of processes and outcomes, given shape and voice by its authors.

What are the ways of shaping proof then? One method is to layer interdisciplinary systems into a complex whole. I have, however, chosen a more convergent approach: rather than separating proof into constituent disciplines of architecture, landscape, sustainability, history, and so on, I group the simultaneities of these research agendas into singular forms that allow multiple performances. In HBNY (Parenthetical Space) project, for example, the premise of programming for multiple users is seen as a new translation of sustainability, where materials and energy use can be reduced through the sharing of a single space. The inaccessible archival storage necessitated by the program requirements for the Czech National Library evolved into efficient spatial volumes that, in turn, physically and symbolically define a new civic space for the city of Prague. Instead of expressing one truth, the proof I seek is activated by allowing minimum form to take maximum effect across the range of interrelated disciplines.

Czech National Library
Prague, Czech Republic, 2006
Competition

As both a secure repository of books and a symbolic public building, a national library must negotiate the spatial dichotomy between storage and display of knowledge. Since major portions of the building must be devoted to publicly inaccessible archive areas that are opaque and hermetically sealed, how can a national library be designed to maintain an inviting civic presence?

In order to distribute the sheer volume of storage needed onto a surface, the book stacks are formed into a curved shell that appears to hover above an urban-scale "mound," which contains archival maintenance and repair programs. Between these volumes a new winter garden becomes an intermediary public space, bridging the urban street edge at the library's front with the historical park at its rear.

The curved form of the upper volume is a long-span truss housing a system of ramped bookshelves and reading rooms that allow new interactive relationships between viewers and books. With what can be described as a constantly changing "light monumentality" during the day, the curved specular surface reflects the surrounding cityscape; at night an internal illumination reveals the massive collection of books and knowledge within.

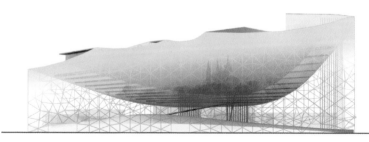

1

1: South elevation: during the day, the interior curved skin reflects the urban landscape and protects the collections from sunlight. 2: View at dusk 3: East elevation: the book stacks are illuminated from within at night.

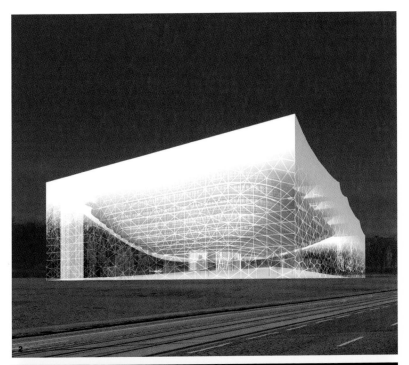

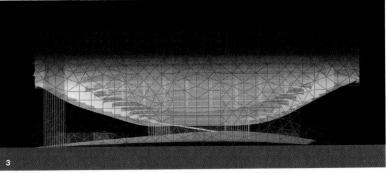

4: The space the book stacks occupy is translated into surface area. Can books become incorporated into the building elevation? 5: Peeling the flat floor plate for book storage space into a three-dimensional surface maximizes the contact area between storage and civic programs.

6: Open stacks: moving along the continuously sloped surface allows linear browsing, while the ramp's shallow slope allows one to move across it for cross referencing.

7: Structural diagram

8: Sustainable strategies

9: Aerial view

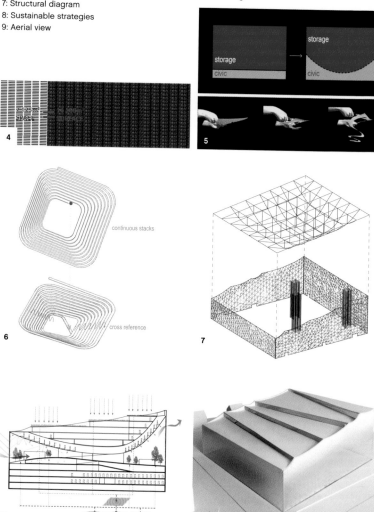

10: The sloping floor of the open stacks allows views into them: the contents of the library become shared cultural property. 11: The rear of the stacks is an organizing apparatus: the user immediately understands that the collection is an open catalog.

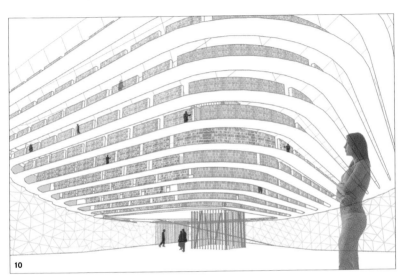

10

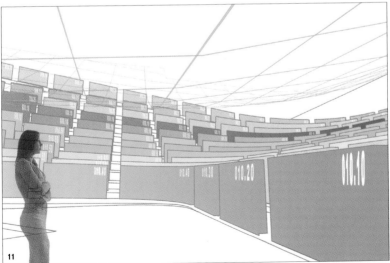

11

HBNY (Parenthetical Space)
New York, New York, 2006
AIA/BSA Interior Architecture Honor Award

The density of today's urban environments is deceptive: while physically substantial, cities can be quite vacant in terms of actual occupancy. Disengaged transactions and interactions between people, places, and events—accelerated by the internet—foster a nomadic lifestyle that not only contributes to material, space, and energy waste but also to the spiraling cost of housing as the available quantity of apartments is artificially diminished. As a prototype for shared metropolitan living, HBNY posits a human-scale solution for this urban-scale phenomenon: operable parenthesis-like dividers and a glass-clad "locker wall" for storing personal artifacts allow twelve on-the-go users to territorialize their changing patterns of habitation and share spatial resources within a single apartment.

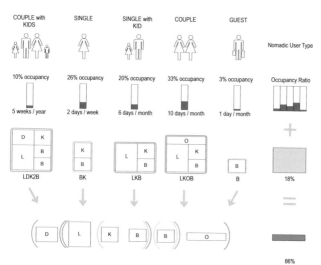

SUSTAINABILITY OF PARENTHETICAL SPACE
By disassembling each residential program and allowing their flexible reassembly, multiple housellolds can share a single apartment as needed. The consequent rise in occupancy rate can reduce material, space, and energy redundancy while helping to alleviate the spiraling cost of housing if implemented as a new socio-urban prototype.

1   HBNY (Parenthetical Space)

1: Nomadic users diagram 2–5: Aluminum mesh curtains provide parenthesis-like dividers for an open space so that users can temporarily customize their patterns of habitation. (Photo: Francis Dzikowski Photography) 6: Plans of curtain dividers

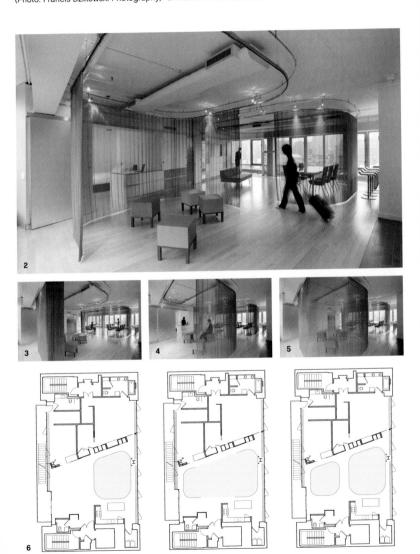

7–10: The way lighting reflects against the mesh curtains creates varying degrees of privacy.
(Photo: Francis Dzikowski Photography)
11, 12: Parenthetical shelving: horizontal adjustability allows various uses and configurations.

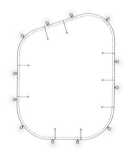

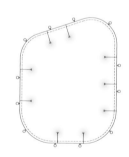

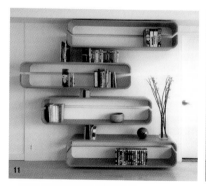

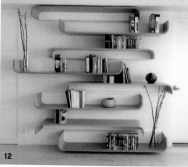

13–15: The locker wall is set at a diagonal to open a wider cone of vision to the skyline from the main living space and the bedrooms.
16: The operable locker wall optimized for carry-on luggage
17: Locker wall in use (Photo: Francis Dzikowski Photography)

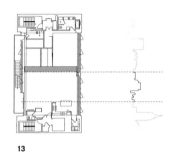

13

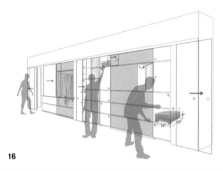

16

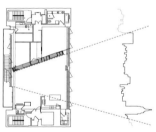

14

15

17

Soft Lofts
Brooklyn, New York, 2006

Rather than assume that urban dwellings must have "hard," shell-like enclosures to address the close proximity of buildings and the public realm of the street, this project proposes a "soft" skin that mediates between inside and outside. Windows, which typically polarize notions of interior and exterior, are made of two layers of operable skin: the outer skin is a clear glass curtain-wall system, while the inner skin utilizes sliding panels with printed "windows" that transition between clear and opaque. The space that is captured between these layers is a soft zone—neither interior nor exterior, but a gradation between the two. Likewise, the sidewall—typically left blank, as only 15 percent of its surface can be open as dictated by code—is conceived as a gradation between opaque and clear. By intermixing concrete masonry units and glass blocks into a single overall pattern, the effect of softness is achieved while following the conventions of the code.

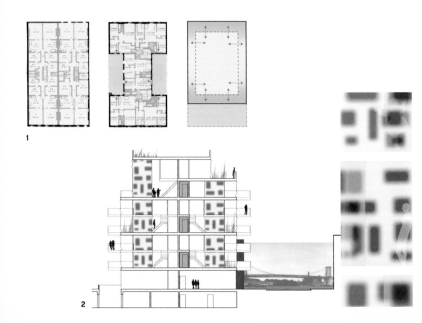

1

2

1: Typological transformations 2: Operable screens with printed "soft" windows allow users to continually change the relationship between inside and outside.
3: The code dictating that only 15 percent of a sidewall can be made up of windows is reinterpreted by creating a pixelated surface comprising glass blocks and concrete masonry units. The gradation between clear and opaque allows glimpses of interior life to animate the wall.
4: View from street

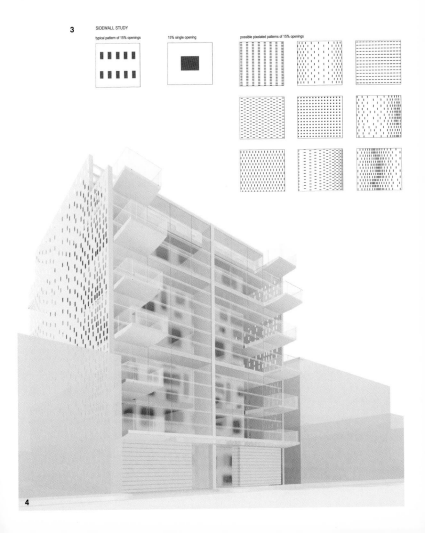

Big Dig Building
Cambridge, Massachusetts, 2004, Metropolis Next Generation Prize, 2005 Holcim Sustainable Construction Award

The Central Artery/Tunnel Project known as the Big Dig is one of the largest construction undertakings in American urban history. A massive amount of waste accompanies construction carried out on this scale—namely the dismantling of the existing elevated highway and the miles of temporary structure used and discarded throughout the project. Public and local governments have remained tacit about the future of millions of tons of materials that must be disposed of as this monumental endeavor comes to a close.

In the same way the urban-renewal frenzy fueled the frantic insertion of the original elevated highway in the 1960s, the equally hasty demolition of this structure forty years later is a convenient bookend to the social and environmental scars it originally caused. The original highway erased massive amounts of existing urban fabric in the name of progress. Likewise, the heroic effort of the current artery project through downtown Boston involves the erasure of miles of reusable structural material. Where the failure of the original highway can now be clearly measured—its unforeseen division of neighborhoods, for example—the downside of the Big Dig's progress is still elusive: it has the potential to negatively impact the environment and economy as materials that contain a high degree of embodied energy are destroyed.

As a palpable alternative to this urban-scale waste, the Big Dig Building is a prototypical proposal that demonstrates that discarded infrastructural materials can be relocated and reused as building components, for uses ranging from structural systems to cladding. Proven highway fabrication technologies can also be utilized to erect a Big Dig Building, drastically expediting the construction sequence. Finally, recycled infrastructure—originally designed to carry the tonnage of cars and trucks—offers the compelling potential to create buildings that can withstand much higher loads than conventional structural systems. In a residential setting, for instance, the ability to incorporate large-scale landscaping into the upper levels of a building is constrained by structural limitations. Utilizing the strength of reused infrastructure, however, allows a more seamless merging of landscape and architecture. This is just one example of how the social ramifications of "heaviness" in relation to "dwelling" can be a new source of innovation.

1: Using salvaged infrastructural materials enables heavy elements, such as trees and soil, of the full-scale landscape to be brought into tight urban conditions.

1

2: Standard vs. Big Dig framing
3: Similar to a prefab system, different typologies can be created out of salvaged components.

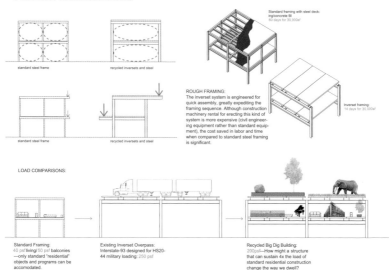

II. COMPARISON OF STANDARD VS. BIG DIG FRAMING

standard steel frame

recycled inversets and steel

standard steel frame

recycled inversets and steel

Standard framing with steel deck-
ing/concrete fill
60 days for 30,000sf

ROUGH FRAMING:
The inverset system is engineered for
quick assembly, greatly expediting the
framing sequence. Although construction
machinery rental for erecting this kind of
system is more expensive (civil engineer-
ing equipment rather than standard equipment), the cost saved in labor and time
when compared to standard steel framing
is significant.

Inverset framing
14 days for 30,000sf

LOAD COMPARISONS:

Standard Framing:
40 psf living/50 psf balconies
—only standard "residential"
objects and programs can be
accomodated.

Existing Inverset Overpass:
Interstate-93 designed for HS20-
44 military loading; 250 psf

Recycled Big Dig Building:
200psf—How might a structure
that can sustain 4x the load of
standard residential construction
change the way we dwell?

2

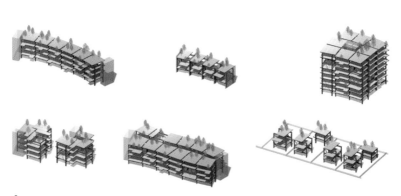

3

4: Cross section 5: Shifting the highway panels creates an elevation that reads as a vertical landscape.

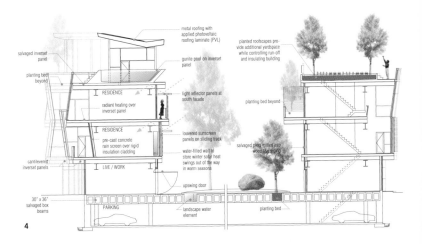

metal roofing with applied photovoltaic roofing laminate (PVL)

salvaged inverset panel

planting bed beyond

gunite pool on inverset panel

planted roofscapes provide additional yardspace while controlling run-off and insulating building

RESIDENCE

radiant heating over inverset panel

light reflector panels at south facade

planting bed beyond

RESIDENCE

pre-cast concrete rain screen over rigid insulation cladding

louvered sunscreen panels on sliding track

water-filled wall to store winter solar heat swings out of the way in warm seasons

salvaged piers milled into wood framing

cantilevered inverset panels

LIVE / WORK

upswing door

30" x 36" salvaged box beams

PARKING

landscape water element

planting bed

4

5

6: Framing of the prototype: using proven highway construction techniques expedites construction from two weeks to only twelve hours.

7: Bachelor pad with large objects, such as pool tables, aquariums, and large-scale sculptures

8: Upper-level family unit with outdoor playground

FRAMING SEQUENCE
The entire structure was framed within 48 hours. Reusing steel structure and roadway panels from the Big Dig makes possible the use of highly efficient infrastructural construction techniques.

6

7

8

9: Duplex unit with rooftop swimming pool

9

Asian Cultural Complex
Gwangju, South Korea, 2005
Competition, Honorable Mention

The act of encircling has both literal and metaphorical meanings. In the context of the city of Gwangju, the historical birthplace of the Korean democratic movement, the act of encircling implies the literal demarcation of a historical precinct within the city's fabric as well as the metaphorical creation of a new public common ground. Encircling is inherently active: its associations include connective movement, community empowerment, and the drawing together of collective experience, culture, and creativity.

The physical form of the Asian Cultural Complex simultaneously allows both inward- and outward-facing experiences of the city. Using the existing Gwangju Fountain—which symbolically marks the origin point of Korean democracy—as its gateway, a new boundary for an urban-scale public park is created. With three historical government buildings at its center, this new open space becomes a place of peaceful reflection of the past's effect on the present. The outer edge of the encircling form becomes a continuous and dynamic place of interchange with the city by providing a porous, nonhierarchical periphery to the urban network of existing streets that converge at the site. Through the use of a new socio-structural form (a structural form that enables greater social interaction), a continuously deflected slab and arch allow reciprocal relationships between the diverse arts and cultural programs within the building. This seamlessness is extended into the urban landscape in the form of a public promenade that merges the pedestrian paths surrounding the building with the vital workings of the complex's internal cultural programs.

1

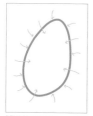   

DEMOCRATIC RING
non hierarchical ring is
approachable from all sides

5 ELEMENTS
plazas signifying the 5 elements
become orientation nodes

HISTORICAL EMBRACE
an urban historical park within
existing urban density

MINIMUM FOOTPRINT
maximum porosity on the public
groundplane is achieved

1: Site strategies 2: Aerial view 3: View from the theater to the green roof: the theater program extends onto the green roof, and indoor and outdoor seating seamlessly merge.

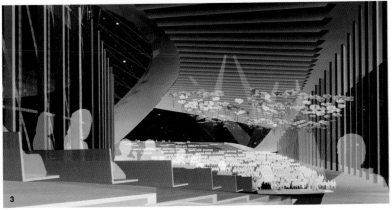

4: Unfolded elevation: a continuous undulating walkway along the edge of the building becomes a linear public amenity for public spectacles and performances. 5: Socio-structural concept: a deflected slab in conjunction with an arched slab creates an efficient long-span structure and sloped space for the theater and assembly programs. 6: Ground-floor plan with five-elements plazas: fire, water, wood, steel, and earth plazas aid in orientation and connect current material culture to ancient Asian notions of nature.

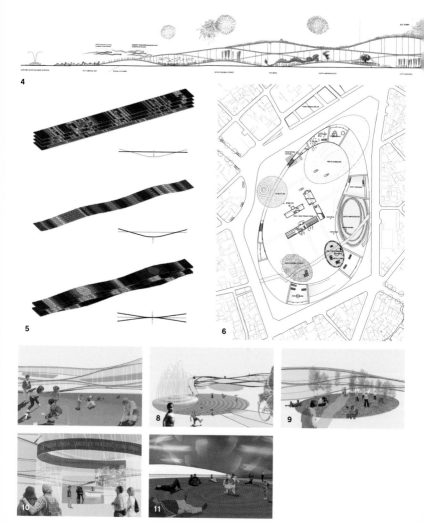

7: Fire Plaza: an interactive-lighting playground serves as an educational metaphor for the fire element. 8: Water Plaza: water surface of the plaza extends the democratic territory of Gwangju Fountain. 9: Wood Plaza: an urban "mound" invites the public to read and rest under a peaceful canopy of trees. 10: Metal Plaza: at the base of the tower, the steel-tube structure serves as "scaffolding" for the display of digital information. 11: Earth Plaza: a sunken theater under the building's arched slabs forms an impromptu outdoor space for events. 12: View from the fire plaza

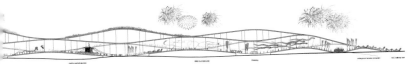

Boston Harbor Pavilion
Boston, Massachusetts, 2005
Competition, Honorable Mention

It is the continuous, perceivable edge between water and land that makes an island an extraordinary natural resource and public amenity. At this intersection, one understands the importance of preserving both elements in a reciprocal equilibrium.

As an urban gateway to the Boston Harbor Islands, this proposal centers around a self-supporting structural roof form that also presents a multilayered analogical and literal reference to the junction between water and land. Whereas excavation is prohibited in the "actual" ground above the Central Artery, the curvilinear roof—reflected onto a polished terrazzo map of the islands—creates an illusion of depth so one can virtually experience the topographic edge where water and land meet. This same roof structure works as a scupper to collect rain runoff for reuse in the bathrooms and landscape, while the way the water is shed off the roof becomes a fountainlike feature for the children's demonstration garden. Interactive visual and audio electronics entertain and educate visitors, enhancing the cafe, bookstore, and pedestrian park programs.

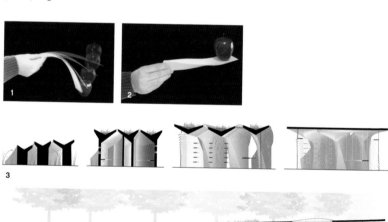

1, 2: Structural roof concept: folding the slab greatly increases its strength. 3: Cross sections 4: Long section 5: The public interacts with the building through both technological and natural means. 6: The transformation of the roof planes from horizontal to vertical creates a continuous transition from public openness to private enclosure. 7: Washrooms occupy the figural sections of the curved structure. 8: Night view

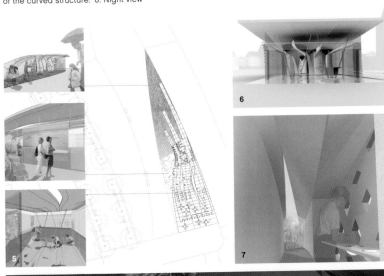

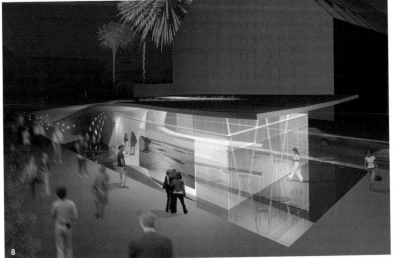

Sponge Park
Seoul, South Korea, 2001
Research

The scarcity of land in South Korea has made the high-rise apartment typology the dominant form of residential building there. A direct result of this density is the elimination of open spaces that promote interaction between residents. Taking a typical housing block as a starting point, a strategy of interventions to integrate park and residence is proposed. Scaffolding, originally utilized in the construction of the building, is reused as a multistory skeletal structure to hold small-scale public green spaces. In this way, the Sponge Park can grow as needed, as public activities infiltrate the tight crevices of the interior space. The result is that the gridlike existing facades transform into a vertical representation of the new connections between previously disconnected apartment units.

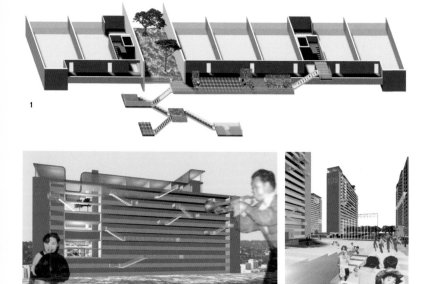

1

2

3

1: Vertical gardens are linked by smaller circulation gathering areas. 2: New "breathing" voids are cut through the existing building, creating community spaces at upper levels. 3: By concentrating parking in tree-covered lots, newly created open spaces, where there was once parking, accommodate larger programs, such as an outdoor theater/garden. 4: Sequential description of Sponge Park

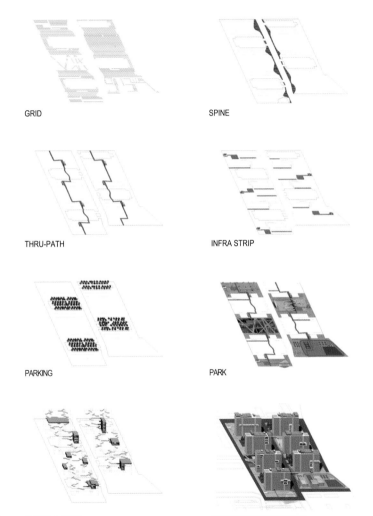

GRID

SPINE

THRU-PATH

INFRA STRIP

PARKING

PARK

4 VERTICAL PARK

LIGHTWEIGHT ROOF UNITS

Aranda/Lasch

128 **Color Shift**
130 **Grotto**
134 **Camouflage View**
136 **Baskets**
140 **Log Cabin**
142 **10-Mile Spiral**
144 **Furniture**
148 **Peninsulas**
150 **The Brooklyn Pigeon Project**

We once built some baskets with a Native American basket weaver named Terrol Dew Johnson and learned that we have much in common. Before meeting Terrol we had always described our approach to design as computational, since we preferred to create our own design tools rather than purchase them. This meant we could use a very fundamental type of language—computer code—to build up our concepts, whatever they may have been.

But our exchanges with Terrol taught us something else. With any technique—whether you call it craft or computation—there exists a certain disengagement from the object being formed, and it becomes about the relationships around that object. Terrol speaks of basket making as a process that brings people together, both those around him as well as the ancestors through which he continues a tradition. He refers to the many voices present in every object—as if each basket is, in essence, a conversation. So, too, we began to think of the making of architecture as connecting themes of universal significance, such as geometry and matter, with the actual experiences of people through which it becomes manifest. It is a boundless and inspiring conversation and reminds us that designing can be a dialogue between two worlds: one entirely abstract and coded, and the other—like the people, communities, and cities we interact with daily— very real and alive. In the end, like those baskets, the truly inspired moment of design comes with the realization that neither of these worlds is of our own making but was always there and somehow discovered along the way.

Color Shift
Queens, New York, 2007

Color Shift is an urban-scaled art project incorporating the FreshDirect video billboard in Long Island City, Queens, the largest LED screen in the United States. We replaced the billboard's regular advertising feed with a continuous stream of slowly changing, saturated colors. The billboard was illuminated for a series of evenings during February and March 2007, transforming the surrounding neighborhood. The effects were recorded simultaneously from different points, and then presented in the gallery at Columbia University's Avery Hall through a three-channel, high-definition video, as well as in large-format photographs. Collaborators include video by Scott Kuzio and photography by Stefan Hagen.

Curated by Mark Wasiuta, funded by Columbia University's Graduate School of Architecture, Planning, and Preservation.

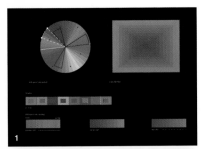

1, 2: Color Shift engine 3: View of the billboard over the FreshDirect facility
4–6: Neighborhood view shown at three different times during the Color Shift sequence:
(green / purple / red)

Grotto
Queens, New York, 2005
Installation proposal for the MoMA/P.S.1 Young Architects Program

The grotto is a landscape element, providing a space of hidden intimacy and pleasure. A proposal for an installation in a museum, the challenge of the project was to invent and develop the structural unit of a grotto, the boulder.

1

1: Folded-paper model
2: South elevation
3: View from courtyard entrance
4: Night view

5: Axonometric drawing
6: Boulder geometry

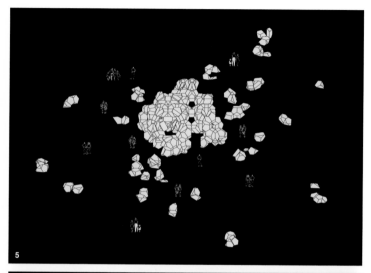

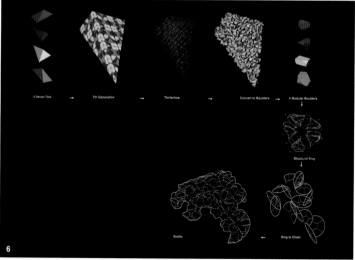

7: Plan view, at eight-foot elevation
8: Plan view, at sixteen-foot elevation

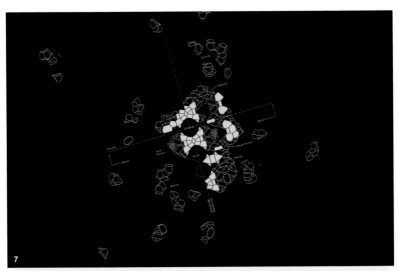

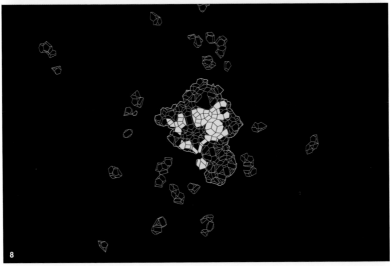

Camouflage View
Grand-Métis, Québec, Canada, 2005
Winning proposal for the International Garden Festival,
Reford Gardens / Jardins de Métis Competition

Take a lovely view and hide it. Camouflage is the art of concealment; it disguises an object in plain sight in order to hide it from something or someone. Through the confusion of foreground and background—a common strategy in animal camouflage—the installation conceals the prized view of the St. Lawrence River from the garden. The view is gradually revealed again as the visitor moves around the piece, making it something to be discovered.

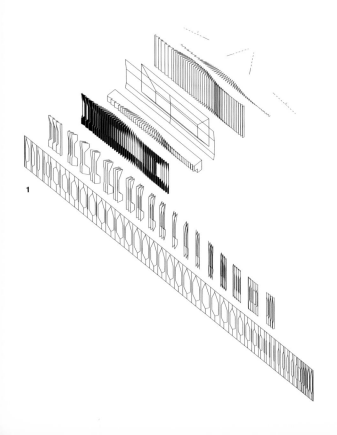

1

1: Axonometric drawing of assembly
2, 3: Front views 4: Fold detail
5, 6: Backside views

Baskets
New York, New York, 2005
Exhibition, Artists Space, Architecture and Design Project Series

Baskets, a collaboration with Native American basket weaver Terrol Dew Johnson, introduces a series of experimental baskets that explore new material and construction possibilities while engaging with the art of traditional weaving. The project connects two distinct cultural practices, basketry and architecture, through their shared foundation of pattern making. In Native American tradition, basketry is a time-honored intersection of cultural tradition and personal expression. In architecture, pattern making has emerged as a generative vehicle for new formal and structural possibilities. Both instances of pattern making reveal the capacity of simple, rule-driven systems, like weaving, to produce a limitless abundance of pattern and form. The collaborative exchange between Aranda/Lasch and Johnson benefits from a rich tradition with ancient roots and has resulted in a series of patterned constructions made from a variety of materials, including grass, wood, glass, and metal.

Curated by Christian Rattemeyer, funded by the New York State Council for the Arts and the Graham Foundation

1: Installation view
2: 444 drawing 3: Endless-knot drawing
4: 444 drawing 5: Conversing-baskets drawing

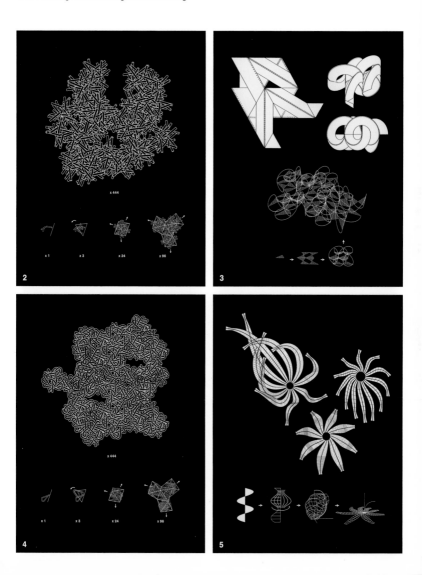

6: Terrol Dew Johnson 7, 8: Basket making 9: Sewing
10: Endless-knot basket

11: Conversing baskets 12: Conversing baskets, detail
13: Knot basket, top view 14: Knot basket, side view 15: 444 baskets

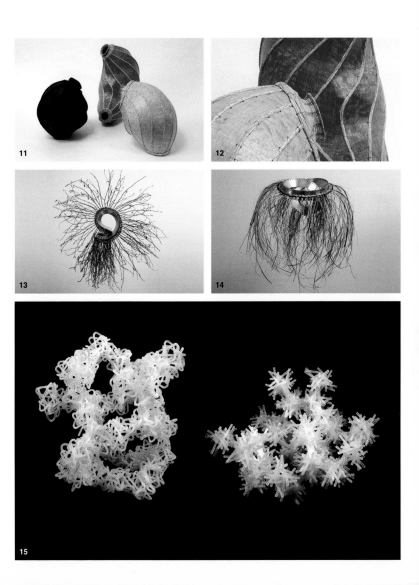

Log Cabin
Palisades National Park, California, 2005
Palisade Glacier Mountain Hut Competition, Finalist

A fire burned down the log cabin that once occupied the project's site. The construction of a log cabin is typically a serial operation of first cutting down trees and then stacking them. What would happen if this order were reversed?
By cutting after stacking—with stacking providing structural stability simply through adjacency—the log's expressive potential is released as it changes shape—from circle, to ellipse, to rectangle.

1

2

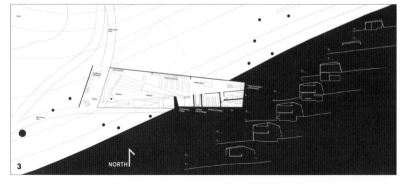

3

NORTH

1: View of north side 2: View of south side
3: First-floor plan
4: Facade-tiling diagrams

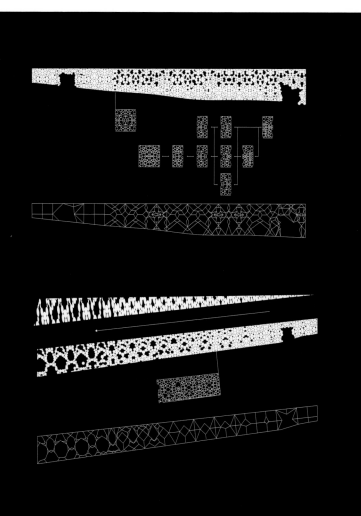

4

10-Mile Spiral
Las Vegas, Nevada, 2004
Vegas Sign Competition

10-Mile Spiral acts as a massive traffic decongestion device for the bumper-to-bumper traffic that occurs on weekends along I-15, the interstate corridor that eventually becomes the famous Las Vegas Strip. It does so by adding significant mileage to the highway in the form of a spiral. It anticipates Las Vegas before one's arrival: along its spiral you can play slots and roulette, get married, see a show, have your car washed, and ride through a tunnel of love—all without leaving your car. It is a compact Vegas, enjoyed at fifty-five miles per hour, with a towering observation ramp that offers views of the entire valley floor below.

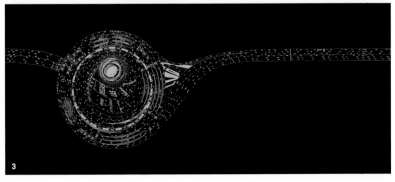

1: Dirty spiral 2: I-15, leading to the Vegas strip 3: Plan-view drawing
4: Leaving Las Vegas 5: On the spiral 6: Observation tower interior

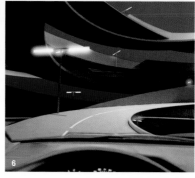

Furniture
Private Commission, 2006–present (ongoing)

Taking cues from the structure of quasicrystals, the Furniture collection is
developed as an aperiodic, three-dimensional tiling system. Like a regular crystal,
the structural lattice of a quasicrystal fills space completely in three dimensions
without leaving any gaps. Unlike a regular crystal, the lattice pattern of a
quasicrystal never repeats the same way twice. The quasicrystal foundation
assures that every piece is modular but never redundant.

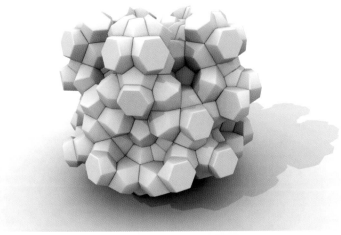

1

2

3

1: Quasicrystal packing 2: Quasicrystal-ring structures 3: Quasicrystal packing
4, 5: Quasi-chair renderings 6: Quasi-cabinet prototype

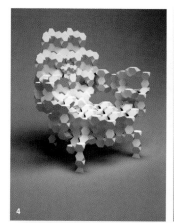

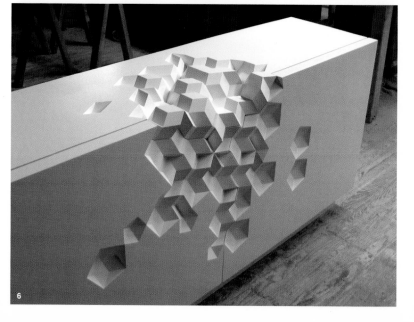

7: Quasi-chair rendering

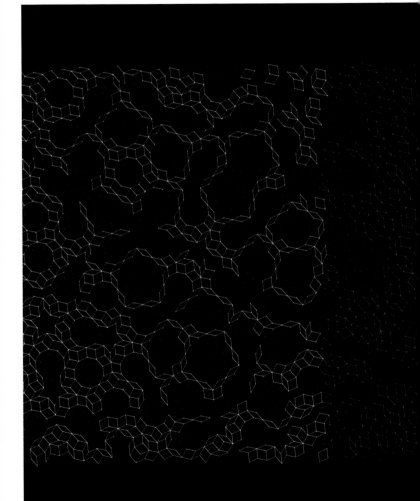

7

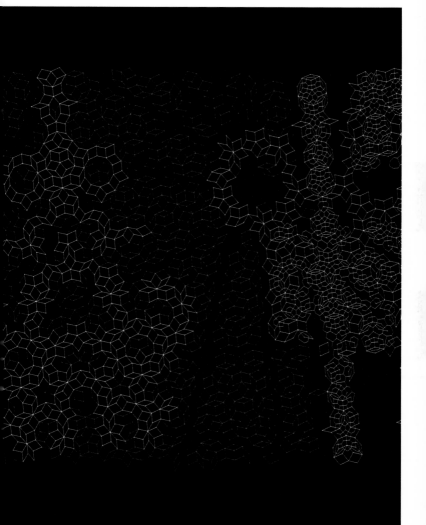

Peninsulas

New York, New York, 2003
Exhibit Design for On Site: New Architecture of Spain,
Museum of Modern Art

Peninsulas is an exhibit system for the Museum of Modern Art (MoMA) show On
Site: New Architecture in Spain. A set of peninsulas—assembled using a three-
dimensional tiling system—displays artwork, paying tribute to Spain's geography
as well as its rich architectural legacy.

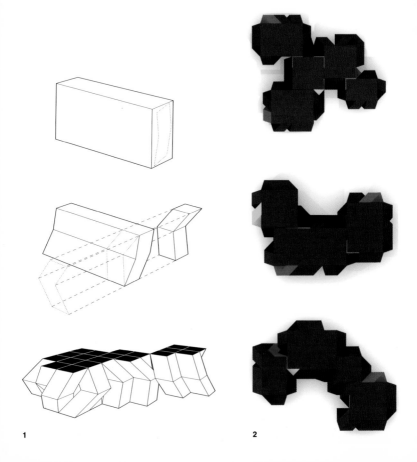

1   2

1: Foam-cut fabrication diagrams 2: Clusters 1, 2, 3
3–5: Installation views

The Brooklyn Pigeon Project
Brooklyn, New York, 2003
Broadcast on PBS, *Reel New York*

The Brooklyn Pigeon Project is an experiment in developing a satellite that
records the city as seen by a flock of birds. Using trained pigeons and working with
seasoned bird flyers, the project team equips pigeons that fly in regular spiral
patterns over swatches of Brooklyn with wireless video cameras and microphones.
Harnessed to these custom cameras and small battery packs, the birds become
satellites carrying "earth-sensing" equipment that feeds images and sounds of the
city back to a ground location. Their flight paths capture unconventional portraits
both of the city below and of flock motions. This unique way to see Brooklyn
contrasts directly with the way the city is increasingly recorded and represented
today. The advent of geographic information technologies and the rise of network
protocols have placed virtually all urban imaging and remote sensing systems
"on the grid." Using a flock of birds as one component of an imaging apparatus,
this project attempts to confront the limits of this grid by creating an equally
rich disclosure of the city: seeing the city as a flock would.

Funded by the New York State Council for the Arts.

1: Rubin, pigeon satellite 2–4: Pigeon-camera footage

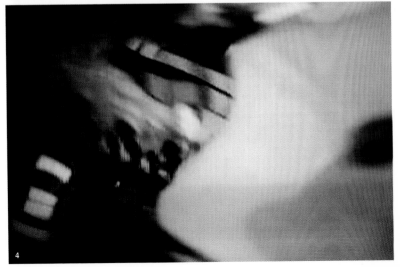

UNI

154 **Design and Development (S, M, L, XS)**
156 **S (Small)**
160 **M (Medium)**
164 **L (Large)**
168 **XS (X-Small)**
174 **+ (plus)**

"Someday my prince will come!" Princess Aurora sings with confidence in *Sleeping Beauty*. There is a prince, and he will come. In reality, especially for young architects, her assertion is more like a speculation: "Someday a *client* will *really* come?"

We doubt that a project will come if we only wait for it. We activate and employ our concepts—we do not sleep and linger. We want to prove that there is an innovative way to quick-start the careers of young architects, to have actual architectural projects instead of years spent waiting. Although new building technologies and systems now exist, the relationship between architect and client has remained static, without many opportunities for fresh possibilities. We try to expand the scope of the architect's role and experiment by wearing many different hats—those of designer, owner, and contractor. The following design and development project is proof that young architects can work within a compound network—developer, contractor, inspector, owner, and architect—to achieve an ideal concept and make it real.

Design and Development (S, M, L, XS)
Building type: two two-unit condominium associations
Location: Cambridge, Massachusetts
Construction dates: March 2003–August 2006
Lot size: 6,000 square feet each
Zoning: residential B (two- to three-family house)

The compound is located in a quiet residential area near Boston, where most houses are built in either the Worker's Cottage or New England styles. S and L are the two original standing structures on the site; XS and M new constructions. Although each of the units has a different configuration and choice of materials, together they form a collective within a single property. The extremely small construction budget (each structure cost between $50 and $100 per square foot) and tight zoning regulations determined the materials and forms. Rather than hiring contractors, we undertook the construction to show that the most basic building materials and construction skills, combined with clever planning, can result in something interesting. We bought many D.I.Y. books, spent hours on the internet researching affordable materials (cork flooring, polycarbonate, plywood, left-over marble tiles), and spent weekends and nights doing most of the work ourselves.

1

1: Site plan of XS, S, M, L
2: View of M (left) and XS (right) from the backyard
3: View in-between L (far left) and S (far right) from the street

S (Small)
Construction dates: March 2003–August 2004
Size: 1,500 square feet (2 bedrooms, 2.5 bathrooms)

The renovation of the first piece of the compound by UNI, S (Small)—nicknamed "Metal Storage" by the neighbors—was completed in 2004. The facade, composed of a two-story corrugated Cor-Ten steel wrapper and translucent polycarbonate siding, retains the contextual identity of the neighborhood with reference to local wood and foliage. Cor-Ten's oxidized surface forms a protective coating, requires no painting, and needs minimal maintenance. The design eliminated the nooks and crannies from each floor to create wide-open spaces, and brings light into the backyard-facing east facade with large windows and translucent polycarbonate walls. The open plan of the house expands the experience of the space, and the white finishes reflect light throughout. White paint, which requires only one coat, was used as a money-saving strategy. One side of the house is a functional wall that contains the utilities, such as the kitchen, baths, and stairs; the opposing side brings light indirectly to the first floor, from a skylight through the slotted opening in the second floor.

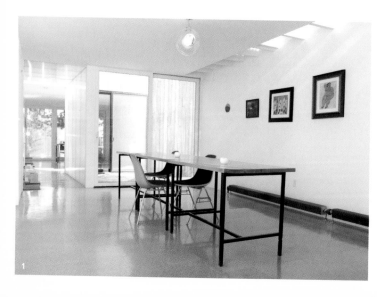

1: The first-floor living room of S, showing the polycarbonate corridor and terrace between S and M. The transition is kept as open as possible to promote the flow of space and allow views to the garden at the rear. 2: S's street-facing west facade

3: Second-floor bedroom of S, with exposed roof collar ties.
4: First floor of S during the construction of M. (S and M were connected later, and the first floor of M became an addition to and extension of S.)

5: A translucent polycarbonate corridor between the renovated S (left) and the new addition M (right) unites the bright lighting and clean surfaces of the two spaces. It also creates an outdoor sitting area for S. 6: Light shines through the polycarbonate panels, concealing the upstairs bedroom.

M (Medium)
Construction dates: October 2004–August 2005
Size: 1,700 square feet (3 bedrooms, 2.5 bathrooms)

The second piece of the compound, M (Medium)—called "Black Box" by
the neighbors—is a twenty-nine-foot-high extension connected to the original
S house by a ten-foot-long translucent polycarbonate corridor. It is a new
construction, completed in 2005, with a tunnel-like open space on each of its three
floors. The cost of M was minimal—inexpensive red cedar tongue-and-groove
siding was used, stained black to hide the blemishes on the exterior.

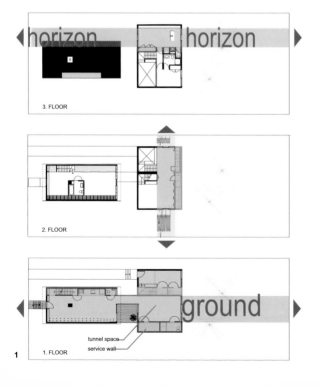

1

1: Spatial diagram for S (direction) and M (direction)
2: M house

3: M during construction
4: Bathtub in the middle of a bedroom on the third floor of M

5: View in-between M (left) and XS (right)

L (Large)
Construction dates: March–September 2006
Size: 2,400 square feet (4 bedrooms, 2 bathrooms)

L (Large)—or "Grandma Shed," as the neighbors call it—is a renovation completed in 2006 that retained its existing cedar-shingle siding. We were able to take out a second mortgage on S after selling M, which allowed the renovation of L. The roof over the balcony of L is conspicuously absent—a trick employed to minimize the total floor-area ratio (FAR) and create a place to relax on a starry night. The typical room distribution of a house was inverted, with the unit's four bedrooms placed on the first floor, saving the second story for the kitchen, family room, and living room. The renovations also eliminated the existing attic and interior walls, creating a more light-filled and flexible space. To stay on budget, we used wood recycled from S to build the closets and old joists found in the basement of L to construct the stairs.

1: L house
2: Terrace behind existing facade of L

2

3: First floor, finished with recycled wood from the basement of L

4: Second floor, ceiling opened up with demolition of attic
5: Basement with original flagstone foundation

XS (X-Small)
Construction dates: March–August 2006
Size: 1,100 square feet (2 bedrooms, 2 bathrooms)

The final piece of the residential compound, XS (X-Small)—also known as
"What the Hell is This?"—is made up of three rotated, stacked sixteen-by-
twenty-two-foot boxes with four-corner skylights. The skylights of the
new construction provide the interior spaces with maximum natural light and
maximum privacy (minimal windows, both in size and quantity, were used),
an important feature considering the proximity of the four houses to each
other on just two lots and the boldness of the house designs. XS is finished in
marine plywood, typically used in boat building. The facade's plywood grain
is broad and pronounced, creating the appearance of a huge piece of furniture.
Each floor of XS has a different look and feel (marble on the first floor, oak
plywood on the second, glass walls and marble in the third-floor bathroom),
but they are all connected by a wooden staircase that threads through
the space.

1: View from the parking lot
2: Exterior view

3: Module concept

MODULE

The module/block is the basic constructive element of the modern home with a panelized building system. It can be easily handled, transported, and stored as either fully-fitted modules or flat-packed panels.

MODULAR CONSTRUCTION

Individual modules are stacked on top of each other. By rotating and shifting modules, multiple skylights can be created to gain more natural light and privacy in narrow lots where homes are located side-by-side.

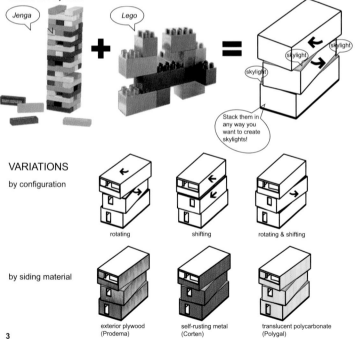

VARIATIONS

by configuration

rotating   shifting   rotating & shifting

by siding material

exterior plywood (Prodema)   self-rusting metal (Corten)   translucent polycarbonate (Polygal)

4: Construction view

5: XS during construction
6: First floor

7: Second floor, with plywood floor and walls
8: Third floor

+ (plus)
Zurich, Switzerland, 2007
Competition entry

+ (plus) is a competition entry for a guest house and restaurant addition
(approximately 15,000 square feet) to an existing dormitory building at
Eidgenössische Technische Hochschule (ETH) university in Zurich, Switzerland.
The programs were divided into two distinct, barlike structures—with the
restaurant on top and guest house on bottom—stacked perpendicularly to
represent the symbol of the cross on the Swiss national flag. The exposed portion
of the roof of the lower volume is a multifunctional outdoor space for the hotel
and restaurant.

1: Aerial view of ETH in Zurich, Switzerland
2: View from the campus showing the existing building and the new + addition at the top of the formal dormitory
3: Interior view of new restaurant at the top level